In the Neighborhood

In the Neighborhood

The Search for Community
on an American Street,
One Sleepover at a Time

Peter Lovenheim

A PERIGEE BOOK

A PERIGEE BOOK
Published by the Penguin Group
Penguin Group (USA) Inc.
375 Hudson Street, New York, New York 10014, USA
Penguin Group (Canada), 90 Eglinton Avenue East, Suite 700, Toronto, Ontario M4P 2Y3, Canada
(a division of Pearson Penguin Canada Inc.)
Penguin Books Ltd., 80 Strand, London WC2R 0RL, England
Penguin Group Ireland, 25 St. Stephen's Green, Dublin 2, Ireland (a division of Penguin Books Ltd.)
Penguin Group (Australia), 250 Camberwell Road, Camberwell, Victoria 3124, Australia
(a division of Pearson Australia Group Pty. Ltd.)
Penguin Books India Pvt. Ltd., 11 Community Centre, Panchsheel Park, New Delhi—110 017, India
Penguin Group (NZ), 67 Apollo Drive, Rosedale, North Shore 0632, New Zealand
(a division of Pearson New Zealand Ltd.)
Penguin Books (South Africa) (Pty.) Ltd., 24 Sturdee Avenue, Rosebank, Johannesburg 2196, South Africa

Penguin Books Ltd., Registered Offices: 80 Strand, London WC2R 0RL, England

While the author has made every effort to provide accurate telephone numbers and Internet addresses at the time of publication, neither the publisher nor the author assumes any responsibility for errors, or for changes that occur after publication. Further, the publisher does not have any control over and does not assume any responsibility for author or third-party websites or their content.

First edition: April 2010

Library of Congress Cataloging-in-Publication Data

Lovenheim, Peter.
    In the neighborhood : the search for community on an American street, one sleepover at a time / Peter Lovenheim.— 1st ed.
        p. cm.
    Includes bibliographical references.
    ISBN 978-0-399-53571-0
    1. Community—United States. 2. Neighborliness—United States. 3. Neighborhoods—United States. 4. Social networks—United States. I. Title.
    HM756.L69 2010
    307.3'3620973—dc22   2009032267

PRINTED IN THE UNITED STATES OF AMERICA

10 9 8 7 6 5 4 3 2

This book describes the real experiences of real people. The author has disguised the identities of some, but none of these changes has affected the truthfulness and accuracy of his story. Penguin is committed to publishing works of quality and integrity. In that spirit, we are proud to offer this book to our readers; however, the story, the experiences, and the words are the author's alone.

Most Perigee books are available at special quantity discounts for bulk purchases for sales promotions, premiums, fund-raising, or educational use. Special books, or book excerpts, can also be created to fit specific needs. For details, write: Special Markets, Penguin Group (USA) Inc., 375 Hudson Street, New York, New York 10014.

In fond memory of
Dr. Louis R. Guzzetta
Dr. Patricia DiNitto
and
Dr. Renan Beckman Wills

———

And to Irina

One must seek out a good neighbor, even more than a good companion.
—Machzor Vitry, commenting on the Talmud, Pirkei Avot
(Sayings of the Fathers), 2:13

ACKNOWLEDGMENTS

For the many hours they spent with me discussing the initial concept for this book, I thank Rabbi Raphael Adler, Rafe Martin, and Mark Kramer.

This book went through many drafts and I am indebted to friends and colleagues who slogged through them and offered their good counsel: Guy Kettelhack, Andrew and June Lovenheim, Robert Lovenheim, Larry Merrill, Susan Kramarsky, Jan Goldberg, Andrea Barrett, Joan Brumberg, David Brumberg, Eli Cohn-Wein, Amy Mantell, Marie Lovenheim, Susan London Gordon, Irina Novozhenets, and Mark Kramer.

I especially thank my friend Byron Rubin, who read two complete drafts and spent many hours discussing with me what might be done to improve things. Patricia McClary also read multiple drafts. Her insight and humor were of great value. Similarly, I thank my late cousin and friend, Herbert Siegel, for his careful reading and excellent editing. As an editor, Herbert was patient, kind, and generous, as he was in life. And to my lifelong friend, Rabbi David Katz, I am indebted for countless hours of stimulating and helpful discussion, debate, and encouragement as we puzzled out together the pieces and direction of this story.

Along the way, I was privileged to engage the services of Sarah

Flynn, writer and editor, whose excellent editorial help both improved the manuscript and sustained me when it was unclear if the book would ever find an audience.

I also thank my Writers' Group, who listened to early chapter drafts and offered suggestions and encouragement: Zena Collier, Kathy Johncox, Marianne Zeitlin, Rahul Menta, Lisa Rubiner, and Gail Hosking Gilberg. And I remain grateful to a few special teachers and editors who taught and inspired me: first and foremost, Clayton O'Dell, as well as Elizabeth Hart, Sandy Tropp, Mary Anna Towler, and Howard White.

Thank you to William Maley, Brighton Town Attorney, for assisting with access to public records; to Tom Low, Brighton Commissioner of Public Works, for letting me view archival sewage inspection footage; and Mary Jo Lanphear, Brighton Town Historian, for helping me learn about the history of my neighborhood. Moreover, I thank Dave, Doug, and Mike McEwen for sharing with me their memories and artifacts of the real Houston Barnard. And thank you to Tony Toscano for his skillful efforts with computerized imaging as I sought to capture an entire street in one photograph.

I'm not sure this book would have been published if my daughter Sarah's friend, Lisa Bonos, of the *Washington Post*, had not turned to me at dinner one evening and said, "This book you're writing about sleeping over at your neighbors' houses might make an interesting essay for the paper." And I thank the Op-Ed Page staff of the *New York Times*—editor David Shipley and Mary Duenwald—for publishing the piece and for their superb editing.

How can I thank the neighbors who opened their doors and their lives to me? I value our deepened friendships; I hope I have honored your trust. Thank you to: Lou Guzzetta, Deb and Dave O'Dell, Jamie Columbus, Bill Fricke and Susan Hyman, and Patricia DiNitto. Also, my thanks to a few neighbors whose stories did not make it into the book, but whose help and encouragement I nonetheless appreciate: Rose-Marie Klipstein, Carol and Michael Yunker, Pat and Irene Burke. I thank Phil Marshall, musician and music therapist, for his compassion toward my neighbor, and that unforgettable bedside rendering of "Love Me Do."

When I began this project, I hoped that out of a tragedy something positive might emerge. For Ertem and Robert Beckman's trust in allowing me to attempt that, I am honored and deeply grateful. To Ertem, Robert, Orhan, Marcia, Peter, and Kendall: thank you. Similarly, thank you to Ayesha Mayadas and Bill Kenny.

That brings me to two people without whom none of this would be possible. My agent, Geri Thoma, who persevered long after others might have given up, and Marian Lizzi, my editor at Perigee— what a privilege and pleasure it has been to work together.

Finally, I thank my children, who always inspire and sustain me: Sarah, Val, and Ben—your curiosity, humor, steadfastness, and love make it all worthwhile. To each other, may you always be good neighbors.

CONTENTS

INTRODUCTION

THAT first evening, as I left the house, the last words I heard before I shut the door were, "Dad, you're crazy!" from Valerie, my teenage daughter. Sure, the sight of your fifty-year-old father leaving with an overnight bag to sleep at a neighbor's would embarrass any teenager, but "crazy"? I didn't think so.

There's talk today about how as a society we've become fragmented by income, ethnicity, city versus suburb, red state versus blue. But we also divide ourselves with invisible dotted lines. I'm talking about the property lines that isolate us from the people we are physically closest to: our neighbors.

It was a calamity on my street, in a middle-class suburb of Rochester, New York, that got me thinking about this. At about 10:45 on the evening of February 29, 2000—the Millennial Leap Day—I was out walking my dog, Champ. We'd gone about halfway around the block when I saw news trucks, their satellite dishes elevated, parked at the end of my street. Police cars and ambulances with red lights flashing were parked there, too. "Some kind of shooting," an officer said. Neither he nor others would say more. I hurried home, told my wife, Marie, what I'd seen, and turned on the television. The eleven o'clock news led with the story: "In the town of Brighton tonight, on Sandringham Road, an apparent murder-suicide . . ." My neighbor had shot and killed his wife, and then himself. Their two young children had run screaming into the night.

Though the couple—both physicians—had lived on our street for seven years, my wife and I hardly knew them. We'd see them jogging together. Sometimes our children would carpool. Some of the neighbors attended the funerals and called on relatives. Someone laid a single bunch of yellow flowers at the family's front door, but nothing else was done to mark the loss. Within weeks, the children had moved with their grandparents to another part of town. The only indication that anything had changed was the FOR SALE sign on the lawn.

A family had vanished, yet the impact on our neighborhood was slight. How could that be? Did I live in a community or just in a house on a street surrounded by people whose lives were entirely separate? Few of my neighbors, I later learned, knew each other more than casually; many didn't know even the names of those a few doors down.

According to social scientists, from 1974 to 1998 the frequency with which Americans spent a social evening with neighbors fell by about one third. Robert Putnam, the author of *Bowling Alone*, a groundbreaking study of the disintegration of the American social fabric, suggests that the decline actually began twenty years earlier, so that neighborhood ties today are less than half as strong as they were in the 1950s.

Why is it that in an age of cheap long-distance rates, discount airlines, and the Internet, when we can create community anywhere, we often don't know the people who live next door?

It was not a fluke that the neighbors involved in the shootings were physicians; many of the people who live on my street are physicians, business owners, and other professionals. I understood that as busy people they valued their privacy; for many, privacy was one of the reasons they had moved here. Indeed, the physical design of our street promoted this. By code, houses had to be set back from the street at least fifty feet. Lots were wide; outdoor activity, if any, occurred in backyards. And as in many suburban neighborhoods, there was no public space to congregate. In short, despite its being upscale, my street reflected the reality on many streets in America today: people were cordial, but they liked their privacy and went about their lives largely detached from those living around them.

And the neighborhood had been that way for some time; I knew it because at that point I was once again living in the house I'd grown up in. My parents had moved out just at the time my wife and I were looking for a larger home, and so we accepted their offer to take the house. I'd been away from the neighborhood for twenty-five years, and in that time, ownership of nearly all the homes on the street had turned over, but as far as I could tell, the neighborhood hadn't changed much; people kept to themselves.

Maybe my neighbors didn't mind living that way, but I did. I wanted to get to know the people whose houses I passed each day—not just what they did for a living and how many children they had, but the depth of their experience and what kind of people they were.

What would it take, I wondered, to penetrate the barriers between us? I thought about childhood sleepovers and the insight I used to get from waking up inside a friend's home. More recently, my family and I had done summer house exchanges with families in Europe—they stayed in our house while we stayed in theirs. After living in these strangers' homes—waking in their beds, fixing meals in their kitchens, and walking in their neighborhoods—we had a strong sense of what their lives were about, something that would have been impossible to achieve just through conversation.

But would my neighbors let me sleep over and write about their lives from inside their houses? In fact, they did, and the understanding I gained—and the lasting connections that were made—validated my hunch that sleeping over would be essential.

In the second year after the murder-suicide, I began to telephone my neighbors and send e-mail messages; in some cases, I simply walked up to the door and rang the bell. Not all my neighbors said yes to my request, of course, but remarkably, more than half of those I approached did. The first one turned me down, but the next one, who lived just two doors down from me, said yes. His name was Lou Guzzetta, an eighty-one-year-old retired surgeon—one of the few neighbors still living on the street from when I'd grown up there. I'd been friends with his son, but had known Dr. Guzzetta only slightly. Now he was a widower living alone.

That was the beginning of a kind of social experiment, a journey of discovery down my own suburban street. (All the principal people are identified, with their permission, most by their real names. In a few instances, I've changed time sequences for narrative purposes.)

Eventually, I met a woman living three doors away who was seriously ill with breast cancer and in need of help. She had recently divorced and had two young daughters. My goal shifted: could we build a supportive community around her—in effect, patch together a real neighborhood?

This is the story of my journey.

1

Waking at Lou's

THE alarm on my cell phone rang at 5:50 a.m., and I awoke to find myself in a twin bed in a spare room at my neighbor Lou's house.

Lou was eighty-one. His six children were grown and scattered around the country, and he lived alone, two doors down from me. His wife, Edie, had died five years earlier. "When people learn you've lost your wife," he told me, "they all ask the same question. 'How long were you married?' And when you tell them fifty-two years, they say, 'Isn't that wonderful!' But I tell them no, it isn't. I was just getting to know her."

At 6 a.m., a grandfather clock on the first floor struck. It played the eight-tone Westminster Chime and then bonged out the hour.

Lou had said he gets up at six, but I heard nothing from his room down the hall. Had he died? He had a heart ailment, but generally was in good health. With a full head of silver-gray hair, bright hazel-blue eyes, and a broad chest, he walked with the confident bearing of a man who had enjoyed a long and satisfying career as a surgeon.

My legs and feet were cold. That was because I was wearing a night shirt. I'd never worn one before, but Lou had made me. All night long it twisted and bunched up around my waist, leaving me half-uncovered.

THE previous evening, when I'd arrived with my overnight bag, Lou had welcomed me right away. He hung up my winter coat and showed me in. His little gray schnauzer, Heidi, yapped and jumped at my feet.

In the living room, Lou sat on the sofa; Heidi lay nearby. He wore a Christmas red, button-down sweater over an olive green polo shirt and khaki slacks. He sipped a gin and tonic. His speech was slurred—frankly, he seemed a little drunk—and he was coughing. The cough, he said, was because he'd started smoking again.

When I had first approached Lou to ask if he'd let me observe him from inside his house as part of a book about how people live as neighbors today, he readily agreed. He warned, however, that there might not be much to see.

"You can write about me," he said, "but it will be boring. I have nothing going on in my life—nothing. My life is zero. I don't do anything."

That turned out not to be true, but I understood what he meant: in recent years, the pace of Lou's life had slowed.

LOU and Edie had six children—five girls and a boy. One daughter, who lived in Portland, Oregon, called that day. So did another, his youngest, from California. Only two of Lou's children lived nearby, both about twenty minutes away. They would stop by to visit, he told me, but more often in the summer than the winter.

"How long can you go this time of year without anyone coming to the house?" I asked.

"Three or four weeks?" he replied.

Lou might have been exaggerating. Later, I observed that at least one of his children who lived nearby seemed to visit weekly. But a week alone was still for him a long stretch of solitude.

Lou once told me he never stayed up past nine o'clock, but at half past nine, we were still talking. I was concerned about keeping him up too late and suggested we turn in. "But tonight I have you here," he said. "I don't want to go to bed." So we talked some more.

He asked if I'd seen a review of the new edition of *The Joy of Sex*. "I bought the original when it came out in—what was it, '72?—at an airport bookstore," he said. "Edie and I were on vacation. They got a big section in it now on AIDS. Now teenage girls call up the boys, ask them for dates, for sex, ba-boom, ba-bah."

"Ba-boom, ba-bah" was Lou's Italian-inspired way of saying "and so forth."

He threw up his hands. "Everything's gone to hell," he said.

At 10:30 p.m., he was ready for bed.

Lou turned off the big-screen TV in the living room, gave Heidi half a biscuit—a "snookie," he called it—and put her in the kitchen, then climbed the stairs, turned off a hall light, and went to his room. That was it. There was no spouse to say good night to, no children to tuck in, no need even to lock the front door because, as he explained, "It's always locked. No one uses it." But for the absence of noise from the TV, my neighbor's house was as quiet after bedtime as it often was during the day.

Upstairs, I asked Lou if I could have a look at his room.

The walls were faded yellow. There was a worn green carpet and a king-size bed. Edie's vanity still stood against one wall. Over it hung a black-and-white photo of her in her thirties, feeding their son in a high chair. Gesturing toward one side of the bed, Lou said, "This is my side. The other side was Edie's. I always sleep on this side because that's where the phone jack is and I'd get calls from the hospital at night."

Until his retirement, Lou practiced as a general surgeon at St. Mary's, one of Rochester's oldest hospitals.

Pointing out the window to a stand of mature trees in the backyard near the in-ground pool, Lou said, "Edie and I planted all those maples." In front of the window, on a coffee table, were Lou's tools for personal grooming—nail clipper, tweezers, cuticle cutter, comb, brush—all set in a row as precisely as a surgeon would lay out his instruments.

I said good night to Lou and went to unpack and go to bed. Lou had given me the choice of any of three empty bedrooms. I'd chosen a corner one on the south side of the house because from one of its windows I could see into my own house. In the room, there was a small black-and-white TV, a shag rug, and two wooden dressers painted fire engine red—probably painted by one of Lou's two daughters who had shared the room when they were little.

I was just opening my overnight bag when there was a knock at the door. It was Lou. He was carrying a gray-and-blue-plaid nightshirt.

"Wear this," he said, holding the nightshirt out to me.

I thanked him but said I'd brought pajamas.

"This is better than pajamas," he insisted. "It's an extra. Take it."

I thanked him again, but said I'd be fine in pajamas.

"Wear the nightshirt!" I could see he wasn't going to take no for an answer. "You can take it home with you."

So I wore the nightshirt.

THE grandfather clock downstairs struck again, this time with a single bong. It was 6:15. Still no sound from down the hall. Maybe Lou was just really quiet in the morning. I opened the door so I could hear better, then went to the corner window.

Both the house next to Lou's, and my house one door down, are contemporary split-levels. They are smaller and, to my mind, less architecturally interesting than many of the other houses on the street, which are more traditional in design. Lou's house is a white Colonial. Looking past the house next door, I could see a small section of the upper floor of my house, including a window in the room of my older daughter, Sarah, who was away at college.

I was just thinking how nice it would have been if I'd brought binoculars when I noticed sitting on a nearby bookshelf a tiny, child's telescope. It must have been from one of Lou's daughters when she lived in this room. I doubt it was more than 10-power magnification, but even so, pointing it at my daughter's window, I could make out a familiar Ringo Starr poster on her wall. Then, lowering the telescope, I saw my own reflection in the dark window glass: a middle-aged man of medium build with thinning, dark hair, in a nightshirt. Nothing so unusual about that, I suppose, except that I'd woken up in my neighbor's house and was looking back toward mine with a spyglass.

In truth, I didn't need that little telescope to see what was going on inside my house; with reasonable certainty, I knew where everyone was: Valerie, my teenager who the night before had accused me of being "crazy" for leaving the house with an overnight bag, was asleep in her room upstairs; Ben, then nine years old, was in his bedroom downstairs; and nearby, sprawled on a sofa in the downstairs den, was our dog, Champ. Champ, a mix of a black Lab and a dachshund, had a Lab's big head and tail, but stood just eleven inches high. And there was one more occupant of my house that early morning: my children's mother, Marie. We'd met in college, married in our late twenties, and enjoyed raising three children together. But Marie and I had made better parents than partners, and somewhere around Year 17 of our marriage, things had begun to unravel. We slogged through a couple of tough years—years that were unkind to our kids—and then separated. By the time of my sleepover at Lou's, our separation had been made legal, and the anger and resentment we'd felt had largely dissipated. People say that the phrase "amicable divorce" is an oxymoron, but in our case—at least after that first year or two apart, it was largely true. Though we were living apart and we each had started dating, Marie and I were on good terms, especially when it came to watching out for the kids. So it was that Marie had offered to stay over that night—a night of the week when Val and Ben were normally with me—so the kids wouldn't be alone. I couldn't be sure, but I assumed, as I peered through that window in the corner room at Lou's house, that Marie was asleep in what used to be our bed.

AT 6:18 a.m., from down the hall in Lou's room came the sound of a loud, almost hacking cough. A minute later, a toilet flushed.

My goal was to meet Lou the moment he emerged from his bedroom, so I'd need to be quick about getting showered and dressed.

In the hall bathroom, I pulled off the annoying nightshirt and started the shower. As I waited for the water to warm, I caught a glimpse of Sandringham Road through a small, porthole-like window. The developer who had carved this neighborhood from farmland more than eighty years earlier had planted each side of the wide street with alternating linden trees and Douglas firs. These trees were now nearly a hundred feet tall. The lindens were bare of leaves that time of year, but the branches of the firs were green and, that morning, heavy with snow.

It's odd to wake up on your own street, look out the window, and see a house across the street that's not the one you normally see. But when I looked onto Sandringham Road from the window in Lou's bathroom, that's what I experienced: in place of the redbrick house across from mine was a white, wood-frame Colonial that stood across from Lou's. It was the home of the neighbor I had approached before Lou, who had turned me down.

IN the shower, I enjoyed a surprisingly powerful blast of hot water. Despite recent laws about water-conserving equipment, Lou probably hadn't changed the showerhead in decades, but I wasn't complaining.

I stepped from the shower to dry off. If I was quick, I could shave and dress before Lou came out of his room.

Done shaving, I pulled on a T-shirt and pants just as, from down the hall, I heard the door to the master bedroom open.

Music, loud music from a radio—a clarinet backed by a

full symphony orchestra—swept out of the room and with it, washed, shaved, hair combed, fully dressed, with a bounce in his step and a wide smile, came my neighbor, Dr. Louis Guzzetta.

"*Buon giorno!*" he called grandly, smiling broadly, arms spread wide. "*Come sta?*"

Come sta? How was I? I was in the upstairs hallway of my neighbor's house at the very moment he was leaving his bedroom to start his day. The fanciful idea that I could penetrate the barriers that separate neighbor from neighbor and get to know my neighbor from inside his own home was coming true. And I could see by the bounce in Lou's step that he was delighted at the prospect of having attentive company all day, and glad to have me there.

"GOOD morning, Lou," I said, coming out of the bathroom. He was wearing the same red button-down sweater, olive polo shirt, and khaki pants as the night before.

"Now, am I allowed to go downstairs by myself," he asked, "or do I have to wait for you to follow me?"

Lou was playfully reminding me that last night I told him I'd want to watch everything he did today. As I finished dressing, I mentioned that we'd have to be careful to avoid the "observer effect," that people often do not behave in the usual way when aware of being watched.

"Yeah, well, I can already see that's true," he said. "I've never come out of my room and yelled, '*Buon giorno!*' I'm putting on a show."

"Well, don't," I said. "Just do what you would normally do, as if I weren't here."

I knew, and I was sure Lou knew, that my presence in his

house couldn't help but affect his behavior. Yet it seemed to me the effect would likely be small. I asked myself: If someone slept over at my house intending to get to know me by observing my normal day, what would I do differently than I normally do? I might dress a little neater, be a little more purposeful in some of my actions, a little more patient with calls from telemarketers, but really, how much different could my behavior be? I'd still do the same things: get up, fix breakfast, read the paper—maybe I'd clean the dishes right after eating instead of letting them sit all day. If I were writing, to make a good impression I might waste less time checking online for news, stocks, and e-mail. An observer would see a slightly cleaned-up version of my day, but 90 percent of it would be accurate. And that's what I figured I'd get with Lou.

"The night shirt bunched up around my waist," I said as I walked behind Lou down the stairs to the kitchen.

"That's because it's not your size," he replied. "I bought it for myself. It's probably an extra-large."

"Really? An extra-large?" I asked. I was surprised because Lou was of average height.

"It's because of this," he said, gesturing to his belly. "*La Bonza!* The abdomen. The curse of the American male. We all get this goddamn *La Bonza!*"

I said, "It comes with age."

He said, "No, it comes with eating."

Lou, at slightly over 200 pounds, had put on considerable weight in the five years since Edie died. "I've outgrown my clothes," he told me earlier. "The days of clothes are over." In fact, I'd seen Lou wearing moth-eaten sweaters, and pants—including the ones he wore that morning—an inch or two short.

Downstairs, Lou let Heidi, the gray schnauzer, out into the fenced backyard. In the kitchen, he opened the refrigerator. A quart of half-and-half he'd bought two weeks earlier had expired. "I used it for Brandy Alexanders on Christmas morning," he said, tossing it in the trash. He took out a bottle of orange juice.

The breakfast table sat in an alcove facing the street. Through sheer cloth curtains I could see Sandringham Road, empty in the dim, early-morning light. "Edie made those," he said, referring to the curtains. On the table, he had lined up four bottles of pills: two for high blood pressure, another for his heart—he had suffered a silent coronary—and a low-dose aspirin to help prevent heart attack and stroke.

Lou stepped outside to retrieve the morning papers and to let Heidi in. Then he set the table. "I don't usually use these"— he meant the white paper napkins he placed beside each of our plates—"I put them out in your honor." He was having cereal and a banana. I said I'd have the same.

Seated at the table, he scanned the local paper, then got up to sprinkle food into a large fish tank on the kitchen counter. "This was Edie's," he said of the tank, which held half a dozen colorful fish. "She knew all about it." Lou said at one point the pH was off and the fish weren't doing well. How, I asked, does he know when the fish aren't doing well?

"They die," he said.

He had put something in the water that was supposed to help the fish, but said when they all finally die, he won't replace them.

Lou returned to the table with a bag of large pretzels, dipped them directly into a soft stick of butter, drank his coffee, and flipped some more through the paper. "Let's see if anyone left us," he said, turning to the obituaries. "Anne Wolf," he said, reading aloud one name that he said sounded vaguely familiar. "No," he concluded after reading the notice. "I don't think I knew her."

"How well did you know Renan Wills?" I asked.

"Name isn't familiar," he said. "Someone I should know?"

I reminded Lou of the murder-suicide down the street. He recalled the incident, he said, "But I didn't know them at all. Never saw either of them. Terrible tragedy. Guy was nuts."

Finished with his coffee, Lou excused himself to go to the garage to smoke. "It stinks up the house if I smoke in here," he explained. He had quit smoking a year and a half earlier but recently had resumed the habit. He said he limited himself to half a cigarette a couple of times a day.

I was puzzled that Lou so easily dismissed our neighbors' murder-suicide with a remark like, "Guy was nuts." For me, it wasn't so simple; there were troubling aspects of that tragedy that I wanted to learn more about. For now, though, with Lou, I let it ride. The morning was going so well; it was the first morning in a long time that I'd shared breakfast with another adult. I liked it, and I sensed Lou liked it, too. We lived so close; I wondered why we didn't do it more often.

A few years later, I thought back to my breakfast that day with Lou, when I read of neighbors in Galveston, Texas, sharing home-cooked breakfasts in the aftermath of Hurricane Ike. The City of Galveston, population about 55,000, sits on Galveston Island on the Gulf Coast of Texas. After the hurricane came ashore, residents of Galveston who had stayed on the island to ride out the storm suddenly found themselves in what journalist

Jennifer Latson termed a "symbiotic alliance." Some found fresh water, some cooked food; others checked on those in greatest need. "They survived," Latson wrote in the *Houston Chronicle*, "as if they were stranded on a desert island, which, technically, they were."

On Ball Street, in Galveston's historic East End, residents, lacking grocery stores, restaurants, or transportation, became "pioneers in their transformed neighborhood." One homeowner, Yolanda Gomez, forty-six, borrowed a twenty-five-year-old propane camping stove from a neighbor and cooked hot meals for the whole block.

"Before the storm, everybody had their own lives," said Gomez, who had never spoken to several neighbors until Ike introduced them. "After it passed, everybody just got together." By the third morning after the storm, the only invitation her neighbors needed was the smell of eggs and sausages to draw them to her porch.

There's something about a terrific storm—or, I suppose, any natural disaster—that brings neighbors together. In a letter to me, Patrick Ellingham, sixty, of Hollywood, Florida, recounted his experience in 2005 in the aftermath of another hurricane. "When Hurricane Wilma knocked out our power for almost two weeks, people started walking around the neighborhood and actually talking to each other. It was interesting how many people knew me by sight but had never spoken to me. We swapped life stories and tips on how to live without electricity. Each day, we would check up on each other. When the power finally came back on, doors and windows closed, air conditioners came back on, and we all went back to our separate lives. I'm almost hoping for another storm so we can all catch up."

I was glad it hadn't taken a hurricane for me to have breakfast with my neighbor. Yet, in a sense, it had, for it was only in the wake of the tragic storm that hit the Willses' home that I'd managed to get myself over to Lou's.

AFTER breakfast and his smoke, Lou went into a corner room at the front of the house that he called the library. Paneled in light pine, the room—just 8 by 15 feet—was dark and cozy. He turned on the television to a program of international news, then lay on his back on a black leather couch. Heidi jumped up and rested her head on his legs.

Bookshelves nearby held bound volumes of medical journals. Lou had already thrown many away. "Nobody wants *Surgical Clinics of North America: Liver, Spleen, Pancreas, 1981*," he told me earlier. On the wall above the couch hung framed high school and college photos of Lou's six children, now ages fifty-seven to forty-two: Cecily, Dianne, Frances, Joanna, Louis, and Mary Lou.

I sat in a black leather armchair in the corner. Often, while walking Champ, I'd seen Heidi standing on this same chair, barking out the window. Now I could see that the chair's cushion was patched with duct tape where the dog's toenails had torn the leather; even the duct tape was so shredded in parts that the cushion's cotton stuffing showed through.

It occurred to me: Lou and I had positioned ourselves in this little room like psychiatrist and patient: he lying on the couch and I seated, with notebook ready, in this high-backed leather chair.

Normally, I sensed, Lou would nap now, but because I was there, we talked.

"I remember as a little boy, going out to visit my grandparents," he began, adjusting the pillow under his head. His father's parents had emigrated from Sicily in 1902, entered the United States through Ellis Island, and settled in a small town outside Rochester. "My grandparents kept chickens and grew grapes to make their own wine. When I visited them, there was no inside plumbing—they had a pot under the bed. In the morning, my grandmother would bake bread and she'd let me make my own loaf."

I struggled to stay focused on Lou's story because, as he spoke, I was flooded with memories of having played in this same room as a boy with Lou's son, also named Lou, who was my own age. By the hour, he and a couple of his older sisters and I would sit on this floor playing cards and watching black-and-white TV.

MY family moved to Sandringham Road in the summer of 1957, just in time for me to start kindergarten in the Town of Brighton. Our move from city to suburb was part of the huge out-migration from cities across the country that occurred from 1950 to 1970, when America's suburban population doubled. I remember that on Sunday afternoons, during the months when our house was under construction, my father would drive us all—my mother, my older brother and sister, and me—to Sandringham Road to check on the new house.

It was on one of those Sunday drives, when we were almost at the house, that we hit something. My father pulled the car over in front of a white house. I watched as he walked up the driveway. He said nothing when he returned and drove us back home without stopping at our new house. Later that night, my parents said our car hit a dog—a white poodle—but that the dog was only injured and that its owner was a doctor who would take care of it. Many years later, when I questioned my father about this incident, he confessed he'd actually killed the dog and that its owner—the man in the white house—was Lou Guzzetta. After we'd moved into our new house on Sandringham Road, my father told me, Lou didn't seem to recognize him as the man who'd hit his dog, so out of embarrassment he never mentioned it again.

Our move to Sandringham was a big step up for my parents, especially my father. While my mother's family had been established in Rochester since the mid-1800s, my father's parents had come over from Vienna and Budapest in 1910. They entered through Ellis Island, brought little with them, and eventually settled in a poor Jewish neighborhood in downtown Rochester. From age nine, my father—the youngest of three brothers— delivered newspapers, hawked peanuts at the ball park, and later sold shoes. After high school there was no money for college, so he worked various jobs until he and his oldest brother, in October 1936, started a commercial printing business.

It's hard now to think of my ninety-something dad as a trend-setter, but he and my uncle borrowed whatever they could to acquire what was then cutting-edge technology: an offset printing press. Their business, Great Lakes Press, was profitable almost from the start. Two decades and three children later, he and my mom were ready and able to leave their comfortably modest home in the city for what my dad described as "a genuinely high-class neighborhood" in the Town of Brighton. "It was immaculately maintained," he said of Sandringham Road. "Even where there was an empty lot, the area between the lot and the street was kept up by the garden association or something." To him, the whole neighborhood looked like "a polished diamond."

Our new house was typical of the period: a contemporary split-level with brick facade, wide eaves, double front door, and circular driveway. Inside, the house projected space-age optimism: bay and picture windows, curved walls, and an open floor plan with an expanse of white ceiling that swept unbroken from one end of the house nearly to the other.

On the summer day we moved in, I watched landscapers in front rake the ground in preparation for seeding the lawn and I saw two boys about my own age riding bikes with training wheels. I didn't know it then, but those boys would become my constant playmates. One, who lived just two houses down, was Lou Guzzetta, the younger.

My new friends and I spent many afternoons exploring other houses in the neighborhood under construction. Most of the houses, like ours, were contemporary in style, filling in the empty lots between older, more traditional homes. My favorite stage of construction was when the stairway to a house's second floor was up, but the outer walls, doors, and windows were not yet completed. This allowed us—after workmen had left for the day—to enter the house, climb upstairs, and toss stray nails from the second floor onto cinder blocks that often lay in the dirt beside the foundation walls. Looking back, I was actually inside many of my future neighbors' homes—even their master bedrooms—before they were.

In those early days, I spent hours playing with Lou's son and daughters, but their father was seldom home. "My father's at the hospital," his son would say with pride. On the rare times I saw Dr. Guzzetta, there was a bit of the "Great Santini" about him. He could be stern, gruff, even scary—a drill sergeant to his six kids who, after school, often had their blue-and-white Catholic school uniforms on as they rushed around the house doing chores. I remember Edie, their mom, was often busy in the kitchen, sometimes harried, but more often quietly patient, gentle, and kind. I'd see her on a Saturday morning announcing it was time to "go to the stores," to me a mysteriously vague phrase but one that would cause all the Guzzetta children to load themselves quickly into her wood-paneled station wagon.

My comfortable upbringing on Sandringham Road continued through 1971, when I graduated from high school and left home. In the next fifteen years, as I went through college, graduate school, and my first employment, I lived in several cities before returning to Rochester with Marie and our eldest daughter, Sarah, intent to raise our children among family.

The decision to move back to Sandringham Road was not an easy one. My dad and uncle had sold Great Lakes Press—after nearly fifty years in business—and soon thereafter my parents decided to move to an apartment. When they offered to sell Marie and me the house, we were tempted; the timing seemed favorable. We'd been living in a three-bedroom house in the city but wanted to be in Brighton for the good public schools, and with three children by then, we were ready for a bigger home.

Yet we had concerns. Though the house was a well-built example of 1950s suburban architecture, it wasn't the style Marie and I would have chosen; our tastes were more traditional. Moreover, though I mostly enjoyed growing up in the house, I was concerned how it would be to return to it as an adult. I recalled one episode of *The Twilight Zone* in which a man returns to the neighborhood of his childhood. I tracked down the episode: "Mr. Horace Ford has a preoccupation with another time," intones Rod Serling, "a time of childhood, a time of growing up ... But in a moment or two he'll discover that memories ... can lead into a special province, uncharted and unmapped, a country of both shadow and substance known as . . . the Twilight Zone."

We didn't want a home of "shadow and substance" and haunting background music; we just wanted a nice place to raise our kids. My parents' house was in good condition and sizable: we imagined soccer games in the backyard, and the basement—big enough for both table tennis and billiards—seemed ideal for teen parties.

Our hesitation was as much about the neighborhood as the house itself. Several times—a weekday evening, a Saturday morning, a Sunday afternoon—Marie and I walked the neighborhood. It was as lovely as ever: sidewalks, old-fashioned streetlamps, tall lindens and Douglas firs towering above the wide street. But we saw few people. Occasionally, someone jogged by or passed us walking a dog; not many said hello. The neighborhood association sponsored an annual "picnic," which we attended, but it was like a formal cocktail party, and fewer than half the residents came. We didn't want to label the whole neighborhood unfriendly, but clearly there wasn't much street life. By that time, we'd lived nearly ten years in the city and were used to a front-yard neighborhood with lots of people and kids around. This would take some getting used to.

We procrastinated. My parents offered to sell us the house at a reduced price. That was tempting, but some of the proceeds from the sale of my dad's business had gone directly to my siblings and me. This left me financially secure and able to buy a nice house in some other neighborhood if I'd wanted to. Yet the possibility of moving back to Sandringham intrigued me. Wouldn't it be a rare opportunity to feel rooted and to raise another generation in the family home? Or would it just be regressive, like moving backward? And how would Marie do living in what had been her husband's family home? We debated the issues for weeks—maybe months—and then my parents offered us the house for free. That settled the question. If it didn't work out, we told ourselves, we could always sell the house and move.

As it turned out, we did have a few *Twilight Zone* moments, such as in the first week back when my daughter asked me to play basketball and I mistakenly ran into my son's room—my old room—to get my sneakers. After a year or two, Marie and I hired a designer and completely remodeled the house. We moved some walls, redid the kitchen and every other room, and painted over the brick on the outside. Then it began to feel like our home.

IT was difficult to reconcile the distant memory of my friend's gruff, scary surgeon-father with the elderly man who was now lying on the couch beside me, quietly retelling the story of his own childhood.

At his mother's insistence, Lou entered kindergarten at three years old, and at five began Catholic grammar school, where he sang in the children's choir.

"Do you remember what you sang?" I asked.

Lou lifted his head off the couch and in a childlike falsetto chanted: *"Kyrie eleison, Christe eleison."*

He excelled in Catholic schools through high school and at sixteen was able to enter the University of Rochester. On the wall across from Lou's couch hung a photo of a handsome, smiling, 160-pound Lou Guzzetta standing in black bathing trunks with shoulder straps—a star member of the university's swim team. Later, Lou attended his father's alma mater, Tufts Medical School, graduating in 1945 at the impressively young age of twenty-three.

I asked Lou how he and Edie met. He got quiet, and then I saw tears. We can talk about it later, or not at all, I assured him. I hadn't meant to upset him.

"No, it's okay," he said. "I can do it."

Edith Pinkerton and he met at the university. He was eighteen; she was nineteen. She was from a blue blood family: ancestors on the *Mayflower*, a Daughter of the American Revolution. "She was a beautiful woman with a touch of the Irish in her face," said Lou. "Mature, musically talented, and loving."

"So why was she attracted to you?" I asked playfully.

"I was charming, fun to be with—I have no idea! You'd have to ask her," he said, and then added, "but it's too late."

They dated for a year, and then Lou asked Edie to a dance. He was surprised when she said she couldn't go. "I thought we were going steady," he said, "but she had another date. Hey, no one craps on the old man! I said, 'Good-bye, lady!'" They didn't see each other for a year, but then got back together. "And that was it," said Lou. "We never looked back."

After World War II, during which Lou served as a surgeon with a Marine Corps artillery battalion in northern China, Lou returned to Rochester to practice with his father.

Office visits were $2; house calls, $5. Lou recalled doing tonsillectomies on children at home. To suck up saliva and blood, he'd hook up a suction device to the kitchen sink. Their practice did well. "I had a lot of confidence in myself even then," said Lou. "I read seven journals a month: five surgical and two general. I was good, and I knew I was good."

Lou and Edie moved to Sandringham Road in 1950. They designed the house themselves. The front and sides are brick-fronted, and painted white. Lou calls it a "contemporary Colonial."

I noticed that Lou's nose was running and asked if he had a cold. "No," he said, "I think it's the cigarettes. They irritate the mucous membranes."

As a general surgeon, Lou did all kinds of abdominal surgery, operated on breast cancer, repaired hernias, and performed hysterectomies. Still lying on his back, he explained a procedure he favored for appendectomies, demonstrating by tracing a line with his finger over his belly and getting animated as he described it. Each month, St. Mary's Hospital published a "surgical score sheet." "It was embarrassing," said Lou. "I did more surgeries than anyone else."

To what did he credit that?

"Talent. More schmoozing—is that the right word?—of the referring physicians. Look, I was good. I knew I was good. What can I say? When that phone would ring at night, it was great. You're talking emergency trauma—gunshots, stab wounds. I always came. I never questioned a call. I loved the hospital, especially at night: the trauma cases, the phones ringing. I loved it."

I could picture a younger Lou Guzzetta dashing out of his house at night, speeding down Sandringham Road to the hospital.

"But then it reached a point," he continued, "I was sixty-three—I just got burned out. I got tired of people, I think. There's a new breed of doctor who doesn't care about the patients. The patients have changed, too. Everyone wants a second opinion." Lou told a story: "One day, this woman came to me with an umbilical hernia. It could strangulate the small bowel. She says, 'I want a second opinion.' I said, 'No, you want a *third* opinion. Your internist gave you an opinion, he referred you to me, and I gave you *my* opinion. So now you want a *third* opinion!'"

Two years later, at sixty-five, Lou retired.

"The hospital put on a fantastic retirement party for me," he said. "There must have been a hundred fifty people there. It was at the Marriott—cocktails, ba-boom ba-bah, the whole bash. They didn't do it for anyone else. I made a speech but it was pretty half-assed. I think I was drunk by that time."

I asked Lou how it had felt to suddenly stop practicing medicine. "You have dreams that you're still operating," he said. "You dream a person comes to you and says, 'You're the only one who can help me.' So you do the operation, but you're scared because you have no insurance and you hope everything goes right. It's a horrible, recurring dream."

THE seat warmer in Lou's Lexus sedan was a welcome luxury on our way to the YMCA that cold January morning. Lou wore tinted aviator-style glasses. I asked what his license plate, WEAK 2S, meant. "It's a way of bidding in bridge," he said, explaining that, after his retirement, he and Edie often played bridge with other couples. "You bid weak twos. It was Edie's preferred way of bidding." WEAK 2S had been on Edie's plate, but after she died, Lou decided to use the phrase on his plate, too. Edie's original plate now hung on the wall in the garage.

Just before 10 a.m., gym bag in hand, Lou strode into the Y. In the lobby, four men, all about his age, greeted him. They seemed to have been waiting for him.

"Hiya, Lou," said a slight, gray-haired man.

"Good morning, Doc," said another.

"How ya feeling?" Lou asked the first man.

"Weak. I don't know," the man answered in a high-pitched voice.

"What are you going to do today?" Lou asked him.

"I don't know."

"You can work out," said Lou. "Do a little on the bike. A slow bike ride will do you good."

These men were all retired: a barber, a salesman, an appliance repairman, and a chemist.

In the locker room, Lou hung up his overcoat and sweater. The men then followed him down a corridor to the "Wellness Center," a large, open room with treadmills, stationary bikes, and other equipment.

Everyone else in the Wellness Center—including Lou's buddies—wore sweats or other exercise gear; Lou alone was in street clothes: polo shirt, khaki pants, and still the tinted aviator glasses. As he walked among the fitness equipment, he stood perfectly erect, hands clasped behind him. Even being overweight—his belt buckle, tucked under *"La Bonza,"* actually pointed toward the floor—Lou cast a handsome, imposing image. This was a different Lou Guzzetta than I had seen just a half hour earlier lying on the couch in his library. This must have been the Dr. Louis Guzzetta who commanded an operating room staff as he removed bullets from people's guts in the middle of the night.

Lou asked a young female attendant to check his blood pressure. Three of his buddies gathered around to watch.

"How is the doctor as a patient?" I asked as the woman wrapped Lou's arm in a cuff.

"He scares me," she said good-naturedly. "He scares everyone. He intimidates them. That's how he got so far, I guess."

At the free weights, Lou did a few arm curls with 12.5-pound barbells. Then a few pull-downs, and a quick circuit on the Nautilus. Somehow, his hair remained perfectly in place.

Lou walked among the upper-body machines, greeting people he recognized. He was like the host at a wedding, checking on the guests to be sure everyone was all right and having a good time.

He encouraged me to work out—I had changed into gym shoes in the locker room—but I said I was just observing. "You got to build up your upper body," he admonished. "Guys'll kick sand in your face at the beach!" I did a few curls with the free weights.

A slender man with thinning auburn hair approached. He was one of Lou's gang. "My wife had that surgery we talked about," he said. "Everything went fine."

"Glad to hear it," said Lou.

Lou did ten minutes on an exercise bike.

"Will this get rid of my stomach?" asked a man riding the bike next to him.

"Nothing will get rid of our stomachs," said Lou.

I noticed on Lou's hands patches of deeply reddened skin, especially on the tops of his hands. I asked what caused it. "That's bruising," he said, explaining that with age the skin thins and the capillaries under it can leak.

"It's also from lifting Edie," he explained. "When she was very ill, she could walk but not stand up. I'd put my hands under her armpits to lift her. What you see is the result of repeated trauma."

Lou had worked out for twenty minutes; now it was time for a coffee break, and then a swim. We headed back to the lobby. The other guys were already there, seated at a rectangular table, each holding a foam cup of coffee.

"Here comes the chairman of the board," announced one.

Lou took the seat at the head of the table.

"Hey, how'd you pull the head of the table?" a buddy asked. "Can't you see what's happening here?" replied Lou with mock pride. "I'm the star attraction." At that moment, I better understood why, when Lou earlier had introduced me as a neighbor who "wants to write something about me," these men all seemed to accept that statement without question, as if of course one day Lou would show up at the Y with his biographer.

The Y's six-lane, Olympic-size pool was busy that morning. In the shallow end, a young woman instructed a dozen elderly men and women in water aerobics. In the deep end, a few women paddled slowly around on flotation noodles.

Lou dove in. He did a vigorous freestyle from the deep end to the shallow end, then swam back to the deep end, where he treaded water for several minutes, talking with a friend.

One of Lou's buddies was the first to be done swimming and dressed and out of the locker room. He was eager to leave because that was the one day each month when he volunteered at the Red Cross. I said good-bye to him, and then to the others. Lou, now out of the pool and dressed, was also ready to leave.

In the car, I asked Lou about the man who volunteered at the Red Cross. "He hands out cookies and juice, sets up tables," said Lou. Somewhat dismissively, he referred to the man as "the ultimate volunteer." On other days, he said, the man stays up all night at a nursing home with dying people who have no relatives to hold their hands. But when I asked if maybe Lou would like to do some volunteer work, he rejected the idea. "That's not for me," he said, and changed the subject. He wanted to tell me about something that happened to him recently at the mall.

"This young girl comes up to me. 'Oh, my car is out of gas'— he used a girlish, pleading voice—'and I have to get home. Can I borrow some money, please?' The stories are all the same," he said, almost snarling. "The addiction makes them become total liars. Total liars!"

I assumed that when Lou talked about that drug-addicted girl at the mall, he was thinking of his youngest daughter, Mary Lou, who lived in California. Earlier, he'd told me about her alcoholism and drug addiction, and his frustration at not knowing how to help her.

The Lexus was momentarily silent as Lou pulled out of the snow-covered parking lot.

"So, what are we going to do? Go to the VA?" he asked, regaining his cheerfulness. Every couple of months, Lou went to the Veteran's Administration to get his prescription medications.

"No, no VA," I said. I knew a trip there was not on his schedule that day. "Just do what you'd usually do on a Monday after the Y."

"I *have* nothing to do," he said. "That's the tragedy of my life."

BACK home, Lou and I fixed sandwiches for lunch. As we seated ourselves at the kitchen table, we both noticed the back of his left hand was bleeding. The wound was in the bruised area we had talked about at the Y. Heidi must have scratched him as she jumped up to greet him when we got home. He put a small bandage on it.

While we ate, I asked Lou to tell me about the various dogs he'd owned over the years. He named several but didn't say anything about one of them being run over. I prompted him by asking directly if any were ever hit by a car, and he told this story: many years ago, on a Sunday afternoon, while he and Edie were at home with friends playing bridge, a man came to the door to say he'd hit their poodle and killed it.

"Do you remember who the man was?" I asked.

"No," Lou said. "I have no idea. It was a long time ago."

Well, that was awkward. Lou was being so open with me—about his childhood, his career, even his daughter's struggle with drugs. And here I was withholding information about his dog. I didn't want to sour our budding relationship, but what was the proper etiquette for telling someone your father killed his dog, especially if your father was still living? I wondered if Lou noticed my momentary grimace—it could have just been the sandwich going down the wrong way. Heck, the whole thing was forty-five years and half a dozen dogs ago. I decided to let dead dogs lie, and said nothing.

On a portable TV on the kitchen table, Lou watched the noon stock report while we finished our lunch.

Afterward, we cleaned the dishes and went to the living room. Lou sat on the sofa and I sat on the loveseat—same positions as last night when we talked before bedtime. Heidi lay under the coffee table, chewing a bone. Lou turned on the big-screen TV to watch a business show, and began paging through the newspaper.

Then he announced he was ready for a nap.

I asked if I should answer the phone if it rang.

"No," he said. "I'll wake up to get it. It would be very unusual if it were to ring, though. Very unlikely."

Now that he mentioned it, I realized the phone hadn't rung since I got there the night before.

Lou turned off the TV. Then he turned it on again. "I need a little background noise," he said.

Within minutes, Lou was on his back on the sofa, snoring. His left hand rested at his side, and on the back of it, where Heidi had scratched him, a spot of blood was visible through the bandage. Soon Heidi, too, was asleep.

I got up and walked quietly around the living room. In one corner there was a baby grand piano painted blue; on it stood a photo of Lou and Edie, waving as they leave for their honeymoon.

Looking at Lou asleep on the sofa, I suddenly realized I could be looking at my own future: alone in a big house, a house where you never unlock the front door because no one uses it, where you keep the TV on just for background noise, and where the phone never rings. At least Lou had enjoyed the main prize: fifty-two years of a happy marriage. Maybe someday, I thought, I could remarry.

I went back to the loveseat and put my head down to try to rest.

HEIDI barked, waking both Lou and me. It was 3 p.m. He seemed groggy as he got up to let Heidi out. When he came back, he was holding a small stack of mail, which he tossed, without looking at it, onto the coffee table. The mail landed next to a drooping poinsettia plant. Earlier, I'd asked Lou why he didn't put up a Christmas tree anymore. "What am I going to do with a Christmas tree?" he said. "Sit here alone and watch it?"

"Lou," I said, "the market is up forty points. You probably made a little money while you were sleeping."

The news didn't seem to lift his spirits.

He headed back to the kitchen and returned with a bottle of liquor in each hand.

"What are we drinking today?" I asked.

"I start with this," he said, raising in his right hand a bottle of gin. "Two ounces with tonic water, and then I'll use this"—he raised in his left hand a bottle of scotch—"for floaters. Want one?"

I said I'd join him but only if he made it weak. I get drunk easily.

"I'll make you one like I make for the girls," he said, referring, I guessed, to his daughters. We both went back to the kitchen.

"The guys at the Y really look up to you," I said as Lou fixed the drinks.

"They do," he agreed. "They wait for me to come in. Did you notice that?"

He sliced a lemon.

"I love those guys," he continued. "They use me—"

"They ask you medical questions?" I asked.

"No, not so much," he said. "They use me to set the tone, get the conversation going."

Lou took two plastic tumblers from a kitchen cabinet and filled one halfway with gin. It looked to me like more than two ounces. I filled my own glass to the brim with water and then emptied it back into a measuring cup. "These are *ten-ounce* tumblers," I told Lou. His glass was filled not with two ounces of gin, but five.

"Well, I make it last," he said. "You'll see."

Lou filled the rest of his glass with tonic water, then poured a weaker drink for me.

In the living room, Lou placed his glass and a bowl of ice on the coffee table. "Old people have to be careful with alcohol," he said. "This is how I control it: I feed the ice in slowly, let it marinate. This way I can make one drink last an hour."

I asked Lou about the woman at the Y who took his blood pressure. She had described him as intimidating. Does he think people see him as intimidating, even gruff?

"I know they do," he acknowledged. "It's a curse. I scare people away. I can be very hurtful with my words. I think it comes from my mother's side. She was a perfectionist. I remember once she bought a Studebaker. In those days, the car dealer would bring a new car to your house. By the time that man left our house, he was crying. Nothing was ever good enough for my mother."

"But with your friends at the Y," I said, "you're the ringleader."

"I've become the focus of five or six guys there," he agreed. "Everyone wants to talk to me. I recognize that. They're not as well educated as I am. Sometimes I'll say a word and realize they don't know what it means. I have to watch out for that. But these guys are all veterans. They've raised families. They're all heroes as far as I'm concerned. I'm humbled by it. They don't realize it, but they do more for me than I do for them, like with my friend Carlo DeSantis."

Then he told me the story of Carlo, who died of throat and brain cancer. "I visited with him at least four days a week," said Lou. "I'd take him shopping, we'd go on photography trips, work in his greenhouse, go to Italian grocery stores, where he loved the sights and smells. That took care of about the first two years of my retirement. Carlo came to depend on me. He felt guilty, but I said, 'Please, Carlo, you're making my life for me.' Then he died."

Later, Lou cared for another man who was ill, a vice-president of Kodak. "I'd go over to his house and play gin rummy. I'd take him to doctor appointments. He died, too."

Lou muted the TV.

"I took care of those two like I took care of Edie," he continued. "She had macular degeneration. I had a pair of glasses made for her with telescopic lenses—the kind cardiac surgeons use for fine work—so she could see the cards when we'd play bridge. She couldn't stand, but once I got her up, she could walk. We put handholds around the house. We did okay. We did better than okay. We did magnificently."

I again asked Lou if he wouldn't want to volunteer to help others.

"No," he said firmly. "The doctor at the VA says the same thing. I'm driving her crazy because I have no interests. I have nothing to do. She says, 'Get involved. Volunteer at the VA.' They're desperate for doctors at the VA."

"Does that appeal to you?" I asked.

"No, volunteering has no appeal to me, but I would do it for individuals. I'd like to find someone I could take care of," he said, adding with a smile, "I could take care of you!"

It was 3:30 p.m. Lou looked through the mail, sipping his gin and tonic. "I waited all day for this . . . garbage, bills!" he said.

He opened one envelope. It was a notice of the annual meeting of the Creekside Estate Homeowner's Association.

"What's that?" I asked.

It was the apartment he bought in California for Mary Lou, he explained.

Lou sipped his drink.

"My problem with Mary Lou is the same problem every father has with a drug- and alcohol-addicted daughter," he began. "If it was Louie"—his son—"I'd shut him off. No money—you're on your own. But with a daughter, you can't do that. Where would she end up, living in the back of her car? Whoring on the street? I couldn't do that. Her sisters and brother say, 'Tough love! Shut her off!' They say I'm an 'enabler,' providing an apartment she can use as a crack house. But I couldn't abandon my daughter."

Lou had tried bringing Mary Lou home, he'd tried forbidding her to come home, he'd tried counseling for her, expensive rehab, giving her money, and the apartment. Nothing had seemed to help.

Lou sipped the gin and tonic.

"Maybe the other kids are right," he said. "But I couldn't abandon her."

That Lou was willing to talk with me about this sad part of his life made me feel closer to him, and reminded me of a story in the Jewish tradition: Two men come out of a tavern after having spent some time drinking together. One drapes his arm around the other and asks, "Tell me, do you love me or don't you love me?" His friend replies, "Of course I love you very much." But the first man objects, "How can you say you love me if you don't know what makes me sad?" From this the rabbis teach that to truly know another person, we must know not only their pleasures and successes but also the sorrows they bear.

AT 5 p.m., Lou turned again to the television. "Let's see how the market finished," he said.

As the TV droned, he went to the kitchen to make another "floater"—water with gin.

"Alcohol is a big problem for older people," Lou said again, settling back on the sofa with his drink. "I had patients with real problems. One old lady got drunk every night."

"Could you go a day without a drink?" I asked Lou.

He shot back, "Why would I want to? What else is there? It buys time for me. All I've got is time, for Chrissake." His speech was a little slurred. "I'm sitting here alone all day. What have I got to look forward to?"

I was struck by the two Lou Guzzettas I'd seen that day. There was the public Lou, the Lou at the Y: well-groomed, charming, caring, dispensing good cheer. I'd seen him like that on earlier outings, too. The previous week, when I'd gone with him to the supermarket, a developmentally disabled man whom the store had hired to help customers load their cars approached us in the parking lot. "You are magnificent, young man!" Lou said in a booming voice. "Everyone says that about you." The man beamed. (Later, Lou couldn't resist adding, confidentially to me: "I got more bullshit than an elephant!") Yet he had done the same thing with the girl at the checkout, joking, and helping the time pass as she scanned and bagged his groceries.

But then there was the private Lou: unanchored since his retirement, lonely without Edie, burdened by his daughter's addiction, trying to fill the hours, trying to drink slowly.

Lou announced we'd be having duck for dinner. He had bought it, as he often did, precooked at the supermarket. That I don't eat meat was not a problem for Lou. "You can eat duck," he told me. "Duck's not meat!"

Lou insisted on preparing most of the meal himself, but asked if I would set the table in the dining room. I reminded Lou I wanted us to eat in the normal way, but he insisted he often does eat dinner in the dining room because from there he can watch the news on the living room's large-screen TV.

When dinner was ready, Lou poured wine for each of us and lit two red candles in the middle of the table. I didn't for a minute believe that Lou normally dined by candlelight on Monday evenings, but I made no further objection; he'd prepared a lovely meal and this was a delightful way to end our day together. Dinner was delicious. Apparently, I still responded obediently—perhaps as I had as a child—to Lou's gruff side: last night I wore the nightshirt; today I ate duck.

The dining room was hung with oil paintings of some of the

family's ancestors. Lou's father, Lou told me earlier, had lived to be ninety-three. Would Lou like to aim for one hundred, I asked?

"Live to a hundred?" he shot back. "I don't care if I go tomorrow or in twenty years. I don't care. I don't give a shit. Why? Because I have no life. With Edie I had a life. Oh, for my children and grandchildren I have a role, but for myself, it's no life. I have nothing."

Could he imagine ever remarrying?

"It will never happen," he said.

I mentioned a woman who recently had been widowed, who lived across the street. Lou said he had occasionally talked to her late husband, and knew her "casually," but repeated that he wasn't interested.

"Trust me," he said. "I am so satisfied, you can't believe it."

Would he ever leave Sandringham?

"You mean because this is a big house? People ask me that question and I tell them, 'This is *not* a big house—twenty-five-hundred square feet; twelve-fifty on a floor.' Anyway, where would I move? I've been to a lot of nursing homes, and they all stink." Lou said he had discussed this issue with his eldest daughter, Cecily, a lawyer, who assured him he will never have to leave the house.

"I'm okay living alone," he continued. "But sometimes if the girls call and I don't answer, they get concerned. Like, I get terrible back spasms sometimes. One time, I was in bed—it was about two a.m. I woke up and couldn't move. Somehow I inched over to the phone, called 911, and told them to call Cecily and Bill and have them come over."

Cecily and Bill, her husband, live in an outlying town about a twenty-minute drive away.

"Did they call her?" I asked.

"Yeah," he said.

"And how long did it take her to get here?"

"Well, she'd been sleeping, of course. It took about an hour," he said. "She came over with Bill and they got me out of bed."

He added, "And she changed the bed."

"Changed the bed?" I asked.

"I was waiting an hour and I couldn't move," he said. "I wet the bed."

Lou's admission startled me. The image of him alone in the house, lying in a wet bed, troubled me.

Returning to the question of whether he'd ever leave Sandringham, I asked Lou how, over the years, he'd liked living in the neighborhood.

"The neighborhood's been fine," he said. "We've had some great people—except for a few here and there."

"But Lou," I said, "you've lived in this house fifty-three years, yet when you woke up at two in the morning and couldn't move, are you saying you had no one to call but 911 to ask them to contact Cecily, who lives at least twenty minutes away?"

I couldn't shake the image of him alone at night on those wet sheets.

"Who else could I call?" he asked. "Everyone's busy doing their own thing. I couldn't call you because I didn't know you then. This is not a neighborhood of neighbors, obviously."

"But you just said the neighborhood's been fine," I reminded him.

"What's fine?" he asked. "This guy across the street now, I wouldn't know him if I saw him. All I know is he drives a Corvette. And there's a woman down the street I know. Well, actually, I don't know her. I talk to her when she's walking her dog. I really don't know her."

"None of them," he continued, "were of any help to me with Edie, with the ambulances coming at night. No one cares; no one wants to be bothered. They are not neighbors in the truest sense of the word. There are no neighbors here."

Lou said he had tried to befriend a family who moved in a few houses down.

"At noon one day I took over a fish fry in a box from some takeout place," he said. "The guy takes the fish and we talked a little and he says, 'You'll have to come over and have a beer,' but I haven't seen or heard from him since."

"How long ago was that?" I asked.

"About two years," he said.

A man devotes his whole life to serving his community as a physician—racing in the middle of the night to pull lead out of people's stomachs—and for that, in his old age, he's left alone, isolated from his most immediate neighbors? Seems like in the most primitive cultures the medicine man would be revered right up until the day he died. But here, amid this affluence, our medicine man can't even get invited for beer in return for a box of fish fry. He sits in a wet bed in the middle of the night because he's got no one closer to call for help than his daughter who lives several towns away. And why didn't the simple act of having a meal together ever occur to me before?

"Lou," I said, "if you wake up at night again and can't move, I want you to call me."

"Now I can call you," he agreed, "and you can call me. We know each other." Then he added, "Do you know how to get into my house?"

I didn't, so he told me which door he keeps unlocked. And I told him where I hide a house key.

* * *

AS Lou and I began clearing the table, for the first time that day the phone rang. The unfamiliar sound was jarring.

It was Dianne, Lou's second eldest daughter. She and her children live in a distant suburb. Dianne is the daughter who most resembles her mother: dark hair, slender, and attractive, she was her college's Homecoming Queen.

Dianne had a problem. She'd leased a car but was over the mileage limit and didn't know whether to continue the lease, buy a new car, or buy a used one.

"Get rid of the lease and find a decent used car for yourself," Lou advised as I finished clearing the table. He told her he'd call tomorrow and help her work it out.

At a few minutes before 8 p.m., Lou said he was going to the garage for another smoke. I sensed he was tired after a day of almost nonstop talking. It seemed like the right time for me to leave.

I picked up my overnight bag, put on my coat, patted Heidi on the head, and thanked Lou for letting me spend the day with him. I left by the side door. As I began the short walk home, I glanced back at Lou's house. The only light visible was the one in the kitchen. From the sidewalk, you can see the cloth curtains that Edie made covering the kitchen window. But you can't see the bottles of Lou's pills lined up on the table, or the bottles of gin and scotch inside the cabinet. You can't see the letter in the living room about Mary Lou's apartment in California, and you can't see Edie's old license plate hanging on the wall in the garage, or Lou, standing alone beside it, smoking half a cigarette. To see any of this, you have to be inside Lou's house.

2

"A Considerable Trauma"

NOT long after my sleepover at Lou Guzzetta's, I came across on the Internet this fragment from a biography of Conrad Aiken, the twentieth-century American poet and novelist: "In his childhood Aiken experienced a considerable trauma when he found the bodies of his parents after his physician father had killed his mother and committed suicide."

That reminded me of the tragedy that had occurred on my own street: when Bob Wills, a physician, killed his wife, Renan Beckman Wills (also a physician), and then committed suicide. The couple had two children: Emily, thirteen, and Peter, twelve.

Aiken, a poet, had won the Pulitzer Prize.

I printed out the item and put it aside. For weeks it sat on my desk. Then, one afternoon I looked up the phone number for Renan Wills's mother; I'd heard she and her husband were now living in town, caring for their orphaned grandchildren.

Hesitantly, I called and introduced myself. I said I'd found something about an American poet that I thought might be of interest to her, and perhaps some comfort to her and her grandchildren. I offered to put it in the mail, but she said she wasn't busy and, if I wanted to, I could come over right then—she lived just a few minutes away.

Before their daughter's murder, Ertem and Robert Beckman, both in their seventies, lived in Point Chautauqua, New York, a small town in the westernmost part of New York State. Robert worked as finance director for Chautauqua County. But after the murder, they bought a house in Brighton—just about a mile from Sandringham Road—so their grandchildren could stay in town and finish at the public school.

When I arrived at the house, Ertem Beckman showed me to a sitting room toward the back. This was a home, I thought, that Ertem never expected to live in with grandchildren she never expected to raise. Books and photographs lined many shelves, but my eye settled on a baby photo on the wall. Below, it said, "Renan Beckman, b. 2001, 6 lb. 15 oz."

I was confused. "This is . . . ?" I asked.

"My granddaughter," she said. "They named her Renan."

This was the baby daughter of Ertem's youngest son, Orhan. He and his wife had named the child after his late sister.

"She's lovely," I said as Ertem and I took seats on matching sofas.

"You brought me something?" she asked. Ertem's voice was pitched high, with a slight accent reflecting her upbringing in Turkey. She spoke slowly and deliberately. In dress and manner, she was unpretentious; she'd fit in on a college campus, maybe as chair of the English Department. Yet there was also something about the way she carried herself that was nearly regal. I didn't think it came from any sense of self-importance, more from worldliness and intelligence.

I handed Ertem the printout about Conrad Aiken, nervous because I was unsure how she might react.

She read it, put it down, and said nothing. I feared I'd made a mistake. Then she thanked me, and said she would keep it for the children when they were older.

"We think these things do not happen to us," she said, her voice quavering but her body remaining still. "We think they happen to other people. But then they do happen to us and we are shocked."

Ertem was born and raised in Istanbul. In the 1950s, she came to the United States, attended college, and met her husband, who was then in business school. Her college major, Ertem told me, was sociology. This gave me an opening to ask about how we live as neighbors today and specifically how her daughter had lived on Sandringham Road.

"Sandringham is the crème de la crème, the most affluent, most upper-crust street in town," she said. "When Renan bought the house there, I came over and looked around and said to myself, 'My goodness.' People on that street drive out of their driveways in the morning and then the trucks come and the little green men—you know, the lawn care people—get out and make an awful racket and then leave, and then there's no one around until the afternoon when the big cars come back at the end of the day."

Did she think Renan had been lonely on the street?

"I don't know if I'd say 'lonely,'" Ertem answered, "but certainly she was somewhat isolated. That night she called her best friend, Ayesha, but could not reach her in time."

"She called who?" I asked. I hadn't heard about Renan trying to reach anyone the night of the murder, nor did I quite catch the best friend's name.

"Ayesha," she said, pronouncing the name EYE-sha. "She was born in India."

"Why was Renan calling Ayesha?" I asked. "Did she think she was in danger?"

Ertem said yes, her daughter had felt some danger. She was calling Ayesha to see if she could go to her house with the children.

"Did Ayesha live nearby?" I asked.

"No, not so close," said Ertem. "Not in Brighton."

Immediately, I thought of Lou Guzzetta—how he had woken in the middle of the night with a back spasm and waited nearly an hour for his daughter to drive in from a distant suburb to help.

"Maybe if Renan had known someone else in the neighborhood," I offered, "she could have found shelter closer by."

I knew this might be hurtful to suggest—that her daughter might not have been killed if she'd been able to go to a neighbor's for help—but I was curious if Ertem had ever had the same thought.

"Maybe if she knew someone in the neighborhood, I suppose so," said Ertem. "Don't you think that everyone really wants to know their neighbors? But that is not how most of us live. We know people, but we speak superficially. To really know another person takes time, and we're not willing to do that. But I do believe Bob would have gotten her eventually."

WITH Ertem Beckman's permission, I spoke with many of Renan Wills's family members and friends. From those conversations, and from documents released—also with the Beckmans' permission—by the Town of Brighton, I pieced together the following account of what happened Tuesday, February 29, 2000—Leap Day—inside my neighbors' house:

The day had not begun well for Renan Wills (pronounced re-NON, like *baton*). A family physician, she needed to get to her medical office, but her minivan, parked in the driveway of her home on Sandringham Road, wouldn't start. At 8:18 a.m., Renan made the first of a series of calls to her best friend, Ayesha Mayadas, a metal sculptor and jeweler. The two had met a couple of years earlier at a local tennis club. But when Renan called her friend that morning, Ayesha wasn't home. Renan didn't know it, but Ayesha had left early on a day trip to Toronto and wouldn't be back until evening. Renan left a message. We know what it said because Ayesha never erased the tape. Renan's low-pitched voice was firm and calm, and she spoke in short, declarative sentences as she might while dictating patient reports.

"Hi, Ayesha. It's Renan. It's early. I guess you guys are already out, though. My battery's dead. I think Bob ran it down or something. I don't know if he'll help me start it. Maybe he will, though. Here he comes. Thanks."

Apparently, Bob did start Renan's van because she arrived at her office in time to see her morning patients.

At forty-three, Renan was a petite woman with dark eyes, a narrow face, and straight, short black hair. The eldest of three children, she had been determined since childhood to become a doctor, and pushed herself to succeed. "Talk about sibling rivalry," recalled Orhan, her youngest brother. "Renan was gifted, way out on the bell curve—many standard deviations above the mean." She graduated high school with straight A's and was a National Merit Scholar. Later, at MIT, she excelled not only academically—graduating Phi Beta Kappa—but athletically, too. She captained the varsity crew, even though she stood just 5 foot 4 and weighed less than 110 pounds. Teammates still remember that when they hoisted the shell onto their shoulders to carry it to the boathouse, Renan couldn't reach it. Medical school took her to Johns Hopkins University in Baltimore, where she completed dual residencies in anesthesiology and internal medicine.

On the last day of her life, Renan saw patients until early afternoon, then stopped home, perhaps for a late lunch. If she had taken the most direct route from her office to her house, she would have passed within sight of Dick's Sporting Goods, a retailer of athletic and outdoor equipment. Renan didn't know it, but six weeks earlier—a week after she had served Bob, her husband of seventeen years, with divorce papers, Bob had stopped at Dick's to buy a Mossberg 12-gauge shotgun.

Renan pulled into the driveway of the redbrick Tudor home at 52 Sandringham Road that she and Bob had bought seven years earlier. Inside the house, she discovered in Bob's upstairs study a note listing their children's names and information on a flight to Colorado leaving early that evening. Bob's parents lived in Colorado; Renan feared Bob was planning to run off with Emily and Peter. If so, it would not have surprised her. Their marriage had a long history of conflicts and betrayals.

They'd met at medical school. Like Renan, Bob was bright and athletic. A large man—6 foot 1 and 190 pounds—he especially liked outdoor sports, such as rock climbing and skiing. Renan and Bob married and moved out West, to Washington State, where Bob would specialize in orthopedics and sports medicine and have plenty of opportunity to ski and climb. Both the children were born there.

But the marriage soon fell into trouble. Bob had difficulty

getting along with colleagues, and then a nanny stole money and accused Bob of demanding sex from her. They moved to another city for a fresh start, but Bob had more trouble at work, and admitted to an affair with a nurse.

In 1996, with both her husband's career and her marriage in jeopardy, Renan insisted they move back East to be nearer her family. They both found work in Rochester, just a three-hour drive from Point Chautauqua, where Renan's parents had settled.

But if the move helped the marriage, it was only temporary. In 1999, following an argument with her husband, Renan showed up at work bruised and asked her nurse to take X-rays. Early the next year, after Renan filed divorce papers, Bob one evening threatened suicide. Renan called 911, but when police arrived, they couldn't find him. Afterward, he said he'd been hiding in bushes behind the house. Some nights later, while Renan slept, Bob stole her ID card and broke into her medical office. He listened to her voice mail and read her diary.

That February afternoon, worried over the note with the children's names on it that she'd found in Bob's study, Renan called her parents. Her mother urged her to come to Point Chautauqua, but Renan declined. Emily and Peter had school the next day and she wanted to stay in town. Instead, she picked her children up from school. After a stop at her lawyer's office, she tried to make a call, only to discover that Bob had canceled her cell phone service. She took the children out to dinner, then to the library to start their homework. From a pay phone, she again tried to reach Ayesha. It was 7:15 p.m. Compared to the earlier message, she spoke faster; the "uh" and "okays" hint at a growing unease.

"Hi, Ayesha. This is Renan. I'll try to call you back later. I'm not at home, okay. I'm out with the kids, uh, I'll call you later and explain. Okay, thanks, bye."

At 7:57 p.m., Renan called again, but there was still no answer. Like the previous message, this one lasted just ten seconds, but she spoke more rapidly.

"Hi, Ayesha. This is Renan. I'm going to try you again in about a half an hour, okay? I hope I can catch you at home. I'm not at home. I don't have a cell phone because Bob canceled it. So, I'll try you again. Okay, thanks."

Later, Emily would tell an aunt, "Mom wanted us to go stay at Ayesha's, but Ayesha wasn't there."

At 8 p.m., Renan called her mother.

"We're going home, Mom," she said.

"Please don't," Ertem pleaded. "Come here."

Maybe the kids began getting tired, or maybe Renan herself was getting tired—she'd been going all day under increasing pressure: a van that wouldn't start, then Bob's note, then a dead cell phone. She put the kids in the van and headed back to Sandringham.

When they got home, Bob wasn't there. Tuesday nights he often went to a friend's home to rock climb in a basement gym. Renan told Emily and Peter to get ready for bed. Emily's room was on the second floor; Peter's was in the finished attic.

At around 9:30, the phone rang. It was Ayesha, back from Toronto. She'd heard Renan's messages and called right away.

Renan told her all that had happened that day, but said she didn't feel physically unsafe and that the kids had already gone to their rooms for the night. Nevertheless, Ayesha sensed that Renan was panicked. She advised her not to confront Bob when he got home. They ended the call around 9:50.

Ten minutes later, Bob pulled into the driveway. Renan went

upstairs to a guest room—she'd moved out of the master bedroom several months earlier. Soon, she smelled smoke. Coming downstairs, she found Bob in the living room feeding their
mortgage papers and other documents into the fireplace.

From her room upstairs, Emily heard her parents arguing.

Renan ran back upstairs.

It was 10:20 p.m.

In the basement, Bob cut the phone wires and, on an elabo-
rate stereo system, put on the soundtrack to the violent science-
fiction movie *The Matrix*, turning the volume up as loud as it
would go. Then he removed the Mossberg 12-gauge shotgun
from its hiding place.

Upstairs, Renan reached for a phone, only to find it was dead.
If she thought now of driving the five miles to Ayesha's house,
it was too late; Bob had pulled the distributor wires off the van.
Renan ran into Bob's study and found his cell phone.

At 10:30 p.m., she went into the bathroom next to her daughter's room, closed the door, and called 911.

Meanwhile, with the music pounding, Bob Wills started up
the basement steps. He wore a rock-climbing helmet with a
headlamp.

Emily, in pajamas, came out of her room.

Her father was coming up the steps to the second floor. His
hands were behind his back.

"Daddy, the music's too loud. Can you turn it down?" she
asked.

Bob said he would, and told her to go back into her room.
But she didn't. She remained standing at the open door to her
bedroom.

"Nine-one-one emergency operator. How can I help you?"

Police say when Renan spoke to the 911 operator, she said she feared for her safety and that of her children, but said she did not think her husband had a gun.

The bathroom door had no lock. Bob pushed it open. He grabbed the cell phone out of his wife's hand and threw it against the floor, shattering it. He stepped back. In the hallway, Emily moved forward toward the bathroom door, but her father reached over and turned her face to the side. Then he raised the shotgun.

Emily cried, "Don't! Don't!"

Renan backed away.

He fired three times.

Bob, perhaps already hearing the sirens of police cars as they raced toward Sandringham, ran back down to the basement.

Emily ran to the attic to her brother's room.

"Daddy shot Mommy!" she cried.

"No, he didn't," said Peter. "He wouldn't do that!"

"Yes, he did! We have to go!"

She meant next door, to the home of an older couple, Jean and Ken DeHaven. Renan once had advised her children that if anything bad happened, they should go to the DeHavens' and call the police.

The children came down from Peter's room, but at the second-floor landing, Peter stopped and went into the bathroom to see if his mother really had been shot. He turned her over, and then he and his sister ran from the house.

The first police officers to arrive saw two children running down the driveway in pajamas, screaming. They asked what happened.

"Daddy shot Mommy!" cried Peter. "Mom is dead!"

It was 10:33 p.m.

* * *

THAT night's television news reports were sketchy, but the next day's reports told the rest of the story:

"When the officers arrived, there was the body of a woman on the second floor of the house dead of a gunshot wound," said an on-air reporter, "and a male occupant at the foot of the basement stairs also deceased from an apparent self-inflicted gunshot wound."

The camera showed emergency medical technicians wheeling a body bag on a gurney down the Willses' driveway to a waiting ambulance.

"As detectives canvassed the three-story home for clues," the reporter continued, "the couple's children were taken care of by next-door neighbors until out-of-town relatives arrived."

The relatives were Ertem and Robert Beckman, Renan's parents. After getting a call, they drove from Point Chautauqua and arrived in Rochester around one in the morning.

The TV camera then panned across the front of the Willses' redbrick home, showing the front yard and front door sealed off with yellow police tape.

"All the commotion on this quiet suburban street," continued the reporter, "lured neighbors outside to find out what happened."

They showed a blond woman, identified as a Sandringham neighbor—I'd never seen her before—standing on the front lawn of her house.

"In the summer they'd be jogging together," said the neighbor, speaking of Renan and Bob. "They just seemed so—everything seemed fine. It just goes to show, you never know what's happening in someone else's life."

*   *   *

MANY Sandringham residents responded generously after the shootings. The DeHavens, the couple next door to whom Emily and Peter had run that night, sheltered not only the children but also Renan's parents. Renan's two brothers, Peter and Orhan, and their wives, Kendall and Marcia, stayed with the Arringtons, the neighbors on the other side. Both neighbors, older couples without children at home, housed Renan's family for a week or more. A woman active in the neighborhood association coordinated meals prepared by volunteers.

The first time I met Ertem Beckman and her husband, Robert, was a couple of days after Renan's murder, when Marie and I made a condolence call at the DeHavens'. The Beckmans sat next to each other on a sofa. Both seemed weighted by a burden so heavy that even if they had wanted to stand, they couldn't. I introduced myself, said how sorry I was, but then couldn't think of much else to say; I hadn't, after all, known their daughter well.

At that time, my marriage was strained, so Marie and I went separately to the Willses' funerals; she went to Renan's and I went to Bob's. I chose Bob's, as I recall, not only out of some strange sense of gender loyalty, but because I figured a lot of people would show up for Renan's but few for his, and anyway, I was curious what would be said at the funeral of a man who had killed his wife and then himself. As it turned out, a lot of people went to Bob's; maybe everyone was curious. The eulogies focused on Bob's youth and professional life, and his love for his children; little was said about his marriage and nothing about its ending. Emily was there, surrounded by school friends. She told a relative she decided to go because she didn't want people to think she didn't love her father. Her parents, I thought, must have done something right to raise a child who could say that at such a tough moment.

* * *

IT was a year or two later when Ayesha Mayadas invited me to her and her husband, Bill Kenny's, home. They lived in the city, a ten- or fifteen-minute drive from Sandringham Road. When I arrived, it was late afternoon.

In the kitchen, Ayesha poured us Indian tea. Born in Calcutta, Ayesha emigrated to the United States with her family in her teens. Now in her forties, she was a petite, attractive woman with wavy, salt-and-pepper hair.

As we carried our tea into the dining room, I noticed two answering machines, side by side. To my question of why she had two, Ayesha said one was the one they currently used and the other was the one that recorded Renan's messages the night she was killed. "I don't know what to do with it," she said in her clipped, British-Indian accent.

With Ayesha's permission, I approached the old machine and pushed the "play" button. We both remained standing.

"You have three new messages," said a prerecorded female voice. "First new message: 'Hi, Ayesha. It's Renan.'" Ayesha backed away from the machine. Renan's voice was low-pitched, firm, and calm. The message continued. "It's early. I guess you guys are already out, though. My battery's dead. I think Bob ran it down or something. I don't know if he'll help me start it. Maybe he will, though. Here he comes."

Ayesha and I stood without speaking as the machine played the other two messages. When they were over, for a few moments neither of us spoke. Could she remember how she'd felt, I asked, when she first heard those messages?

"I sensed Renan having a frantic need to get hold of me," she said, recalling that she'd been out of town that day on business. Ayesha came home in mid-evening to find the light on the answering machine flashing. "She must have felt so isolated, just frantically trying to reach me. I sensed something was up, but I still had no idea to what extent—that Bob would be capable of that degree of violence."

Ayesha called Renan back and was able to speak to her, and sensed that her friend was panicked. Then around 11:30 p.m., another friend called to say there'd been a story on the TV news about "something going on on Sandringham."

"We drove there," recalled Ayesha, "parked at the end of the street, and tried to walk up to the house, but the police wouldn't let us pass. Bill asked. 'Is anybody dead?' But the officer wouldn't say anything. We asked if the problem was at number fifty-two. We told him we knew the family and there were kids in the house, but he still wouldn't give us any details. Finally, Bill got hold of a captain and told our story and they asked us to come to the police station."

The police put Ayesha and Bill in separate rooms and asked them both to give sworn statements. In their accounts, they described the history of their relationship with Bob and Renan Wills. Later, they filled in some of the details for me.

Ayesha and Renan had met at a private tennis club in Brighton where both had taken up the game, in part as an outlet from shaky marriages. "There were a lot of women in their early to mid-forties going through relationship issues," she explained. "It was a big escape." Later the husbands met, and the four got on well. They went out often, each couple aware of the other's marital problems and trying to be of help. They went to restaurants, museum openings, and parties. In the summers they dined at the Willses' home and swam in their backyard pool. Once, they all went to a charity ball: Bob Wills rented a limo for the evening; the men wore black tie, the women wore gowns.

Ayesha's husband, Bill, later recalled, "Renan could seem at times a little awkward socially, sort of stiff with forced smiles and laughs. It was awkward, but kind of charming, too. I mean, you're an MD, you're studying your whole life, so where's the time to learn to socialize? Bob, on the other hand, was really a hyper guy. You'd be talking and he'd sit a little too close and look you right in the eye and repeat what you'd just said. He had this constant intensity; he'd never quite chill out—and he was aware of it, too. Once we went hiking at his family's condo in Vail—just him and me—and he said to me, 'Spending three or four days with me—I got to hand it to you, because I'm a hard guy to be around.'"

At around 3 a.m. in the police station, an officer brought Ayesha and Bill together and told them what had happened. "An officer reached over and grabbed my hand," remembered Ayesha. "He said the kids were okay and at a neighbor's. Then we just went home."

Later, after the funerals, Ertem Beckman gave some of Renan's dresses and tennis outfits to Ayesha, and the rest to Goodwill. As we sat at the dining room table with our tea, I asked Ayesha if she still had any of Renan's clothes. She excused herself to go upstairs and a couple of minutes later came down carrying a sweater and two dresses on hangers. She said she had more of Renan's clothes upstairs, including the tennis dresses.

Before laying the clothes on the table, Ayesha pressed them to her face. "They still smell of Renan—perfume-y," she said. There was a sweater Ayesha said she'd worn twice, and two dresses, which she hadn't worn at all. "I can't throw them out, though. They're like the answering machine; I don't know what to do with them."

We talked some more, and eventually I put to Ayesha the question I had been wondering about: if Renan had had a close friend in the neighborhood, might she have found shelter that night?

"It's possible, yes," she said, "although that person might have been put at risk. But I didn't get the sense she knew anyone in the neighborhood." Ayesha referred to the many times she had been to Renan's house, especially in the summer at their backyard pool. "I never saw any neighbors. I don't think she knew anyone much beyond saying 'hello.' As far as I could tell, the relationship of Renan and the neighbors was nothing, it was nonexistent."

THOUGH Sandra Arrington had lived on Sandringham Road for twenty-eight years and I for ten, we'd never met. So when we did meet, as planned, one afternoon at a bookstore café, our initial hello was tentative as we made sure we were both indeed meeting the right person.

I wanted to talk with Sandra because she and her husband had been Renan and Bob Wills's next-door neighbors.

At sixty, Sandra was a slender woman with brown curly hair. She told me she hadn't been close to the Willses, had known them only "in passing." When the Willses had moved in next door, she recalled, she had "tried to initiate conversation" with Renan, but didn't sense any inclination on Renan's part "to know us as neighbors."

"I say that as an observation, not a judgment," she said.

Sipping coffee, she continued, "I'm a friendly person, but if

I don't get an overly warm reception, it remains a "hi-bye" relationship. Anyway, when Renan told me she was an MD, I began making assumptions about how busy she was."

Nevertheless, from her kitchen, which faced the Willses' garage, Sandra became familiar with their schedules. "When Renan or Bob left the house, I'd see their cars going in and out. I knew the rhythm of their lives." Sometimes she'd see Bob and Renan out in front, near where a tall hedge separated the two houses. "Renan was always complimenting Bob about the hedge he took care of," she recalled. "'Nice job on the hedges, honey!' It seemed excessive when I overhead it." She also could see them in the back, at their pool. "We knew they spent a lot of time in their pool," she recalled. "On the weekends, it seemed like they were in the pool morning till night."

I asked Sandra if she had seen the police car at the Willses' house on the night several weeks before the murder when Bob threatened suicide and Renan called 911. She said she had not.

On the day of the murder, however, she did see something: "Between four and five p.m., I saw Bob race out of his driveway. The speed was unbelievable. A red flag went up for me; I thought something was wrong."

That would have been about the time Renan, who earlier that afternoon had picked up Emily and Peter from school, was at her lawyer's office. Apparently, Bob had stopped home while she was out.

Later that night, Sandra saw the aftermath of the shootings. "I looked out the window," she recalled, "and saw lots of lights [and] fire trucks, and called my husband to look out with me. Later, we saw the body bags go out."

I asked how, after the shootings, she and her husband had decided so generously to open their home to Renan's family. "When somebody dies," she said, "you tend to feel helpless. There's only so many things you can do. We have a large house"—the Arringtons' three children were grown and living on their own—"and we consider ourselves hospitable, so when the family began to arrive, it seemed natural to offer them a place to stay."

As it turned out, Sandra Arrington would also have another role to play.

In midlife, Sandra had made the decision to enter the clergy. Though raised a Catholic, she eventually found her way to the Episcopal Church and, at the time of the shootings, was Senior Associate Rector at a church in Rochester—the same church, coincidentally, to which the Willses belonged. "They were parishioners," she said, "although what I would call 'marginal' members—they only came at Christmas—so I didn't know them as members of the church."

Sandra conducted the memorial service for Renan; the pastor later conducted Bob's.

Though by that time she had six years' experience in the clergy, Sandra had never officiated at a service following a homicide. The Book of Common Prayer, she found, had two services, but "they in no way addressed a murder." Given also that Renan's mother, Ertem Beckman, was nominally a Muslim, Sandra decided to look elsewhere for a text. It was in a prayer book from New Zealand that she found what she considered an appropriate liturgy: rites and rituals for a "hard" death.

I wondered, if she were to give a sermon on neighborliness, what would she say?

"Well," she began, "it means to be responsible for each other. You have to say, 'You're my neighbor and I'll do anything to help you,' not just in times of crisis, but every day, and to affirmatively offer that help. And you have to reach out to know your neighbor, to know the rhythm of your neighbor's life enough to know when something is wrong."

She paused, and then added, "However, I'm not sure these days many people are interested in knowing another person that well."

Sandra's comment, coming as it did in the bookstore café, reminded me of something I'd been hearing lately from a number of people: that public space today has largely been privatized. That is, private commercial spaces, like video stores, supermarkets, and chain bookstores are the new "public spaces," and if you want to meet people, that's where you tend to go.

Yet looking around the café that day, I couldn't help but think that if that was the new public space, it was—at least in one important respect—a weak substitute for the neighborhood park, commons, or corner store of old. True, seated nearby were a dozen or more people reading, talking, or working on computers, and some of them seemed interesting enough. Were I bold enough to strike up a conversation, the best outcome might be a new friend. But that new friend was unlikely to be a neighbor—not in the way Sandra had defined it: a relationship of reciprocal responsibility based on physical closeness and the potential need for mutual aid. Making a new friend at a bookstore—remote as that possibility actually was—would not create the kind of close-at-hand support nor the pleasure of casual, daily social contact that only a neighbor can provide. And as for Sandra's question about whether "people are interested in knowing another person that well" these days, the irony was that if anyone here in the chain bookstore was likely ever to "know me" in a meaningful sense, it was the store itself. Through its record of my purchases on its store discount card, the chain knew more about me, what books I read, what music I listened to, even what beverages and cakes I liked—indeed, even the "rhythm of my comings and goings"—than any actual person I was likely to meet there.

Before we finished, I had one more question for Sandra: Despite everything she and her husband had done after-the-fact, did she feel any opportunities had been missed in dealing with the Willses' situation?

"No," she said. "I don't feel that I missed an opportunity. It was a classic case of people being secret. We had no idea what went on inside their home. But when the opportunity presented itself, I think I played my role.

"Now," she continued, "if you're asking had Renan known anyone better, could she have run over to them? Yes, things would have been different. If she'd called me and said, 'Bob's going off his rocker and I need a place to go to,' then of course I would have taken her and the kids in. She might have gone to the DeHavens', too. It's obvious it all could have been prevented. If she'd come over and said, 'I'm afraid,' I would have said, 'Stay here.' I might have insisted."

JEAN DeHaven and her husband, Ken, were in the early stages of cleaning out their house when later I came to visit. Empty nesters, they would soon be leaving Sandringham to move to a town house. Framed family photos and paintings were stacked near the front door, although many others—including oil portraits of their son and daughter—still hung on the wall over the main stairway.

Jean sat in the living room on a plain sofa that she said had been the first purchase she and her husband had made nearly thirty years ago when they married. She was dressed casually, and her hair, short and graying, fell to the top of her wire-rim eyeglasses. Her unpretentiousness distinguished her from many of the women on Sandringham. Perhaps it reflected her upbringing in southern Ohio, where she grew up on a farm.

When the Willses moved in next door, Jean took cookies over to welcome them, and invited them to dinner. Later, her husband, a leader nationally in sports orthopedics, invited Bob Wills, a younger practitioner in the same field, to play golf. "Ken says you can always tell about a person by how he conducts himself on the golf course," said Jean. "But after playing with Bob, he felt they had nothing in common, which was ironic because they had so much in common."

Although Jean often saw Renan out gardening, the two women did not become close. "I didn't know her well," said Jean, "not on a social basis. We were of a different generation, too." Jean did get to know the Willses' children, however, particularly Emily. "Emily had a sitter after school and liked baking brownies. Every couple of weeks she'd come over to borrow things: eggs, a stick of butter, chocolate."

I asked Jean if she sensed any trouble in the Willses' household.

"Not in the least," she said, shaking her head.

The night of the shootings, recalled Jean, she and Ken were watching television when Ken heard a loud crack, but they dismissed it as nothing. "This is an old house," she said. "We hear so many noises."

But soon after, the doorbell rang. Ken got up to answer it, looked out the peephole, and saw Peter and Emily Wills dressed in their pajamas.

"Ken opened the door," recalled Jean, "and Emily blurted

out, 'My daddy has shot Mommy and has shot himself and my mom's dead!'"

I asked Jean how she reacted.

"Evidently," she said, trying to recall, "it was just 'Egads!' and all you can do is hug these kids and pull them away from the door." Jean said they could already hear sirens, and then the police came.

"Emily knew our house was a safe haven," said Jean. "I knew the kids, and Renan had told them that if there was ever a problem, this is where they should go. I asked Emily," she continued, "'Who can you call?' and she said she knew her grandma's number. She called them around 11:30. She was emotional, breaking down and crying. Later, Peter was saying, 'I hate my father! I hate my father!' Ken and I tried to stress, 'This is not your father. This is your father emotionally sick and you hate what he did. He loved your mother and he loved you, but he was emotionally sick and couldn't cope.' All I could do was hug them both and say, 'Your father wouldn't do anything to you and it's an awful, awful, awful thing he's done, but he was emotionally sick.'"

Ertem and Bob Beckman arrived at the DeHavens' a couple of hours later. They, along with Emily and Peter, spent the night there in two empty rooms upstairs. "There was a whole section of the house we weren't using," said Jean. During the night, she recalled, Emily and Peter remembered their two cats. "I'm allergic to cats," said Jean. "But I told them, 'Well, if you don't mind keeping the cats in your room and the door closed, let's go get them.' The police went to get the cats. I think they found one cat and brought it over."

Meanwhile, television news began reporting on the shootings. "The TV talked of an orthopedic surgeon on Sandringham Road who had killed his wife and himself, and they showed pictures of our front door," recalled Jean. "Our friends were getting concerned and calling."

Jean attended both funerals. She said she made a special point to go to Bob's. "Not only did [the Willses] lose their son, but they lost their son in absolutely the most horrible tragedy—he did this horrible, horrible thing. They had to feel as bad as Renan's parents. It was a difficult service to handle. The family ended up just talking about Bob as a wonderful child and young man who had such promise, and they got him married and then—what happened? I think they could have acknowledged what he did and perhaps the mystery of how emotional sickness affects people's behavior."

Ertem and Bob Beckman and the kids and the cat all stayed at the DeHavens' for the better part of a week. As a result, anyone who was close to the family—and all the neighbors who responded by bringing food—were aware of how much Jean and Ken DeHaven did to help.

I suggested to Jean that their last name was appropriate. "You and Ken really were a haven for Renan's family."

"Anybody would do exactly the same thing," she said. She paused, then added, "We knew tragedy. Our son, David, died in '96." That would have been just four years before the Willses' shootings.

"That shock, when you first hear of the death of anyone close, it's like nothing else," said Jean. "But when Emily and Peter came to our door, we could not fathom what they were going through. When we lost our son, our sense had been that we had suffered the worst possible loss—but we had our son for twenty-six years, and he had a good life. But to lose your parents when you are that young, when parents are so important, it's unfathomable."

I told Jean about something that I'd seen on our street a few weeks earlier that had been bothering me. Driving home one evening, I noticed that parked outside a house near the end of the street was an ambulance. I casually knew the family who lived there. They were a professional couple with two children and once had had me to their home for dinner. But I had no knowledge that anyone in the family was ill. What troubled me was that despite thinking about the question of how we should relate to each other as neighbors, I still didn't know what to do when I saw that ambulance. Should I call my neighbor and ask if everyone was okay? Could I perhaps be of help? Or would I be invading their privacy? And what if the problem wasn't illness but domestic abuse, or a teenage eating disorder, or an attempted suicide? Wouldn't my call, in that case, be intrusive and unwelcome? I didn't call that evening, thinking that perhaps I would call the next day—let a little time go by. But the next day came and went and I still didn't call. I never called. And when I happened to see this neighbor walking down the street a few weeks later, I didn't mention having seen the ambulance.

Having lived through the Willses' shootings, I wondered, what would Jean have done after seeing that ambulance?

"I would not have called either," she said. "It would feel too intrusive. But if you ask me, I think not calling would be a mistake. It would not be good. We have to make those calls. If we don't, we could miss someone, someone in need."

So do you think we have any special obligations to our neighbors just because they are physically close? I asked.

"Yes," said Jean, "because they are your neighbors and you're in a position to see things, to know things"—she glanced toward the Willses' house—"but I didn't see anything."

Jean paused.

"Yes," she continued. "You look kindly on your neighbors, and you look after your neighbors. Why? Because they're in your living space, and you want your living space to work well and be healthy."

SOMETIME later, while he was in Rochester for Thanksgiving, I had the opportunity to meet Orhan Beckman, Renan's younger brother. We sat at a restaurant near his parents' home. The resemblance between him and Renan was clear: both were slender, with dark hair, narrow faces, brown eyes, and heavy brows.

Orhan, thirty-six, lived in Vancouver, Washington. A PhD in industrial psychology, he worked at Hewlett-Packard as a "human factors" engineer, helping design new products for ease of use. He was the youngest of the three Beckman children, younger than Renan by twelve years. Growing up, he had, as he put it, a "mother-son" relationship with Renan, at least until she became a real mother when Emily was born.

On the night of the murder, while on a ski vacation with his wife in Utah, Orhan received a call from his mother. "She and Dad were on their way to Rochester. She said, 'I think Renan is dead. Bob shot her.'"

Orhan and Marcia flew to Rochester the next morning and moved into the Arringtons' home next door; later that night, Emily came over from the DeHavens' to stay with them.

"I don't know what we would have done without the support of the neighbors," Orhan reflected. "Food, places for family members to sleep, transportation. It made a horrible situation a little more bearable, and let my mother connect with family and friends without worrying about other things."

Yet Orhan acknowledged that his sister had been isolated in the neighborhood. "I know she felt isolated," he said. "There were some neighbors who knew of and had met her, but I didn't get the feeling that neighbors knew her as a person or knew them as a family. I think she found her community in the tennis club.

"So we're left with the what-ifs," Orhan concluded. "What if Renan knew some of her neighbors beyond a superficial level and could have found shelter with them that night?"

Still, there remained the fact of the neighbors' kindness after the shooting.

"Yes," Orhan agreed, "and therein lies the paradox of the neighborhood's positive response after the fact."

And then, as a psychologist, he lapsed into professional jargon, only some of which I could jot down and understand.

"It speaks to the latent need that isn't addressed without a strong enough stimulus," he began, "which is sad. Because another need that was there before was not met. Relationships in the neighborhood existed, but weren't fostered or developed until there was a tragedy. Then they matured very quickly. The response after the murder was what I hoped would have happened before the murder, and didn't."

Then he said something that was all too clear: "That the marital relationship could fester and steer so far off course in this picture-perfect setting without anyone taking notice—until the results are so obvious that you can't *not* react—is a sad statement on the way we live today."

And what way was that? I asked.

"Ours is a society that favors appearances. If you drive down Sandringham Road, you think, 'Oh, they all have perfect lives: perfect lawns and houses, good jobs and families.' But look more closely. There's no place to go just hang out and talk. My yard becomes a barrier between myself and my neighbor, and neighbors can have little or no contact for years. If you run into someone it's just 'hi-bye.' If you look at it as a case study, what does it say about what could be happening in *any* neighborhood?"

That lack of street life and contact among neighbors is a component, Orhan explained, of what sociologists call "social capital." As distinct from financial capital (money) and human capital (labor), social capital refers to the network of contacts and relationships people have with those around them. Robert Putnam, author of *Bowling Alone*, describes social capital as "connections among individuals—social networks and the norms of reciprocity and trustworthiness that arise from them." Australian social scientists Jenny Onyx and Paul Bullen call it "the basic raw material of civil society." Simply put, if you know your neighbors, greet them on the street, keep an eye on their house for them, or invite them to dinner, this builds connections that in good times can enrich your sense of community, and in bad times can give you someone nearby to call for help.

Social scientists have attempted to measure the level of social capital in different types of neighborhoods. One study asked residents of five neighborhoods questions such as: "If you were caring for a child and needed to go out for a while, would you ask a neighbor for help? Have you visited a neighbor in the past week? In the past six months, have you done a favor for a sick neighbor?" Another suggested a correlation between low social capital and illness when people lack access to immediate, nearby support, and suffer stress from isolation.

As Orhan described it, Renan and Bob Wills had virtually no neighborhood social network. No one on Sandringham had known them well enough to notice their marriage "fester and steer so far off course"; no one had noticed police cars at their house, or if they had, no one checked in with Renan to see if she was okay; and at the crucial moment, Renan had no one nearby to call, and nowhere to run. Her social capital, invested in the tennis club and perhaps with colleagues at work, was of no help; even Ayesha, her one close friend, when she returned to town that night, was five miles away.

Still, there was the neighbors' generous response after the shooting. I asked Orhan how he squared that with such low social capital.

"Perhaps high social capital is proactive and preventive—it helps prevent tragedy," he said. "But low social capital is reactive—it only reacts to tragedy."

ORHAN and I were still talking in the restaurant when the front door opened and Ertem and Robert Beckman walked in. Ertem wore a heavy, gray winter coat. I could almost feel the weight; not only of the coat, but of the sorrow she carried. With them was Orhan's wife, Marcia. She was holding the hand of a little girl who had blond, curly hair, and wore a pink coat, jeans, and sneakers. They all came over to our table. Ertem said they were going to get hot drinks, then go to the canal and feed the ducks. I'd met everyone in the family except the little girl. Orhan introduced me. He said, "This is my daughter, Renan."

3

Footprints

IN the years when I was growing up on Sandringham Road—the late 1950s and '60s—people didn't exercise in public the way they do now. You didn't see adults jogging, biking, or power-walking on the street.

Except one. Nearly every day, a thin, middle-aged woman of slight build walked rapidly through our neighborhood, usually with her head down. No one knew her name, so we called her The Walker. I'd be sitting with my family at the kitchen table, which faces the street, and my mother would say, "There goes The Walker," and my brother and sister and I would look out the window to see. Or I'd be playing baseball with my friends and someone would say, "Hey, there's that walking lady."

Even as a kid, I could tell The Walker didn't live on Sandringham because she didn't dress at all stylishly. I mostly picture her in a simple blue or yellow dress and I remember when it rained she would wear a clear plastic raincoat with a hood pulled over her head. In the winter I think she wore a long, cloth coat, also with a hood; in driving snow she'd cover her face with a scarf.

I admired The Walker. She was out in public, in all kinds of weather, keeping fit. I also felt sorry for her. She always walked alone; I never saw anyone stop to talk with her. I think once, when I passed her on the sidewalk riding my bike, I said a weak "Hi," but I don't recall if she said anything back. I tried to imagine what kind of life she had—where she lived, who her family was, and why she spent so much time walking on our street.

When I moved back to Sandringham as an adult, I was amazed to see that the same woman was still walking through the neighborhood. How old she was at that point was hard to guess.

Then one afternoon—not long after my sleepover at Lou Guzzetta's—I was pulling out of my driveway just as The Walker passed my house. She walked with a limp. Resolved, finally, to meet her, I drove a few houses down the street, parked the car, and walked back in her direction. I approached her in a casual way so as not to startle her.

"Excuse me. I just wanted to say hello," I began.

She stopped. She looked older, smaller, and frailer than I had imagined.

I continued, "I've lived on this street a long time and have always noticed you walking."

"Yes," she said. "I've been walking here a long time."

Her voice was shaky, but she spoke with a clear diction. She said she'd walked in the neighborhood every day since 1960.

"You've walked on this street every day for more than forty years?" I asked.

"I didn't miss many," she said, smiling.

I noted her limp. She said last fall while walking she had

stepped in a hole "maybe a foot deep" between the sidewalk and the street. "It hurt like the Dickens!" she said. "I crawled across the street to my car—luckily no other cars were coming—and drove myself to the emergency room."

She had broken her left ankle in three places and was transferred to a nursing home. Eleven days later she was sent home with a wheelchair, a walker, and a cast. When the cast came off, she started walking again.

Her name was Grace Field.

"In just over one more year, I'll be ninety," she told me. We walked a little together and talked, and then I told her I was writing a book about the neighborhood and asked if she'd be willing to talk with me about it sometime. I said I could visit at her home or we could meet for coffee. Grace invited me to her apartment, which was just a half mile from Sandringham, the next morning.

GRACE said she had had to crawl across the street to her car. The street is thirty feet wide. How long might that have taken? Five minutes? Fifteen?

If there's a place where an elderly woman with a broken ankle crawls across a street and no one notices, and a middle-aged woman is shot dead in her home and no one's life is particularly affected, is it fair to call that place a "neighborhood"?

In the Hebrew Bible, the word most often translated as "neighbor," *rea*, can mean variously: friend, tribesman, fellow Israelite—pretty much anyone not a close relative or foreigner. "Love your neighbor as yourself" (Lev. 19:18), therefore, is a broad injunction to treat kindly most of the people we encounter daily. But *rea* also has the narrower meaning of a person living nearby. "A close neighbor is better than a distant brother," advises Proverbs 27:10. (On the other hand, it's probably just as well I hadn't seen this other bit of wisdom [Prov. 27:17] before I began the sleepovers: "Visit your neighbor sparingly / Lest he have his surfeit of you and loathe you.")

In the New Testament, Jesus is asked, "Who is my neighbor?" (Luke 10:25–37) and answers with the parable of the Good Samaritan. In so doing, Jesus broadens the concept of "neighbor" to include everyone of goodwill who acts with compassion toward another. In this sense, anyone who might have helped Grace Field the day she fell would have been, by definition, her neighbor.

But no one did.

Our English word "neighbor"—derived from "nigh" (close by) and "boer" (farmer or dweller)—takes as its primary meaning the narrower definition: a person who lives nearby. Yet in general usage, the word retains its broader connotation—a neighbor can be anyone who is in relationship with us as part of the larger community. That's what we understood Mr. Rogers to be asking each day on his TV show: "Won't you be my neighbor?"

America itself was partly built upon the concept of people living as neighbors. "If the first foundation of New England's strength and growth was godliness," writes Alice Morse Earle in *Home Life in Colonial Days*, "its next was neighborliness ... The neighborly helpfulness of the New England settlers extended from small to great matters, and entered into every department of town life." Puritans built their settlements around land shared by all members of the community; in New England villages, to foster social interdependence, homes were located within easy walk of a common meetinghouse. For generations after that, we knew our neighbors. Homes had front porches. People borrowed a cup of sugar. The milkman, egg man, and bread man came daily, exchanging news and helping knit together the fabric of a neighborhood.

That model of close dwellings and neighborliness—whether in villages, towns, or cities—largely persisted right up until the early part of the twentieth century when, perhaps in reaction to the stresses of industrialization, Americans embraced a new concept in their choice of dwellings: not "social interdependence," but autonomy. And this new desire for autonomous living was soon reflected in the detached, single-family homes of suburbia. In *Suburban Nation*, architects and town planners Andres Duany, Elizabeth Plater-Zyberk, and Jeff Speck theorize that the roots of the single-family, suburban home can be traced to earlier westward expansion and the "pastoral dream of the autonomous homestead in the countryside . . . to the manse on the agricultural estate, or the cabin in the woods." The new suburban developments were designed for people to live independently, each in his own self-sufficient home, dependent only on cars and roadways to take him wherever he needed to go.

While the greatest explosion in suburban growth would occur after World War II—when the GI Bill, federal home loans, and government highway projects would entice young families out of the cities and into new suburban housing—in fact, development of the suburbs began much sooner.

In the early 1900s in Rochester, New York—as in communities across the country—local and state governments began to lay miles of new roads, sewers, and gas and electric lines. Real estate companies responded by building new subdivisions—new neighborhoods carved from previously rural land. One of these developers was Houston Barnard, a successful engineer and builder. I'll say more about Houston Barnard, the man, later, but

I want to note here that the neighborhood he built, and which still bears his name, was part of that first wave of suburban construction in America.

Barnard started with a few modest subdivisions on the border of Rochester and Brighton, and then around 1918 began what probably he intended as his crown jewel: in the words of one of his ads, "an important real estate enterprise of high character and residential purpose." That would later include Sandringham Road, my childhood home, and again my home as an adult.

Historian and social critic Lewis Mumford, in his book *The City in History*, surveyed the single-family homes of suburbia, and remarked on what he termed "families in space."

"[T]he greater the isolation of the individual household, the more effort it takes to do privately . . . what used to be done in company, often with conversation, song, and the enjoyment of the physical presence of others."

WAS my family, growing up in Houston Barnard's subdivision in the 1950s, a "family in space"? Pretty close to it, as I recall. I don't remember knowing many families on Sandringham other than those of my two boyhood friends, one of whom was Lou Guzzetta's son. We three spent time inside each other's homes, but nearly every other home on our street was, to me, occupied by strangers. I remember playing inside some of those homes when they were under construction, but once the families moved in, I don't recall meeting any of them.

Those childhood memories of being so separate from the neighbors gave me pause about moving back to Sandringham, until my parents, as I've noted, made an offer we couldn't refuse. Still, even after I'd moved back and had begun the sleepovers, I sometimes would stop and ask myself what I was doing: if I knew from experience the neighborhood was largely one of "families in space," why was I so intent on getting to know them?

I don't think it was by chance that I conceived the sleepovers only a year or two after my wife and I separated. At some level, I likely was trying to replace the sense of family I had lost with the split. Yet that would not explain another fact: even before my then-wife and I moved back to Sandringham, when we lived in a friendlier, "front-yard" neighborhood in the city, I had actively sought to connect with the neighbors. I recall discovering a city-sponsored "toy library," and though I could easily afford to buy toys for our young children, I borrowed tricycles and slides, enjoying the sense of community that for me such borrowing represented. I also found a "tool library"—designed, I'm pretty sure, for city residents less able to afford their own drills and power saws than I was, but still I borrowed tools just because I liked the concept. Once, when new neighbors moved in and told us they planned to build a six-foot fence in between our yards, I expressed concern that the fence would cut off our kids' access to each others' play spaces. In response, we agreed on a "mediated" fence: one that was six feet high between the houses but then sloped down to three feet high in the back and inset with a gate so the kids could see into each others' yards and easily move back and forth between both houses. Another time, when a neighbor and I were each growing tomatoes on either side of a chain-link fence, I proposed running my drip irritation hoses under the fence to water both crops at once, in exchange for a small plot in his garden where I could put some extra plants. I liked these arrangements; they made me feel connected to the people around me.

Some of my motivation may have just been leftover communitarian feelings from the 1960s—I'd come of age in the '60s and certainly had absorbed some of that period's notions of community. At another level, though, I may have been after something deeper: as a young child, coming in birth order nearly a decade after my oldest sibling, I didn't quite feel a full part of the family. Perhaps, in whatever neighborhood I found myself, I was always searching for that sense of belonging.

These thoughts were not conscious, however, when I began the sleepovers, and it took the murder-suicide to shock me into going out and deliberately meeting the neighbors. Nor had I thought deeply at that point about what defines a neighborhood, and whether a place where no one comes to the aid of an old woman crawling across the street deserves to be called one. I just knew I wanted to get to know the people nearby.

THE first thing I noticed when I visited Grace Field's apartment was her collection of souvenir spoons: hundreds of little spoons were laid out in fan shapes on coffee tables and end tables, and displayed in boxes hung on the walls. She had many more in storage, she said.

Grace lived alone. One brother lived in Tennessee and another had died seven years earlier. Nearly all of her friends had died, too.

We sat facing each other in big armchairs in the small, carpeted living room. Up close, Grace looked even more fragile and tinier than when I saw her on the street. "I used to be five-two," she said. "Now I'm five even—a little osteoporosis." Her weight, which had long been about 92, had dropped to 85. She had a slight hump on her back. She had short, curly white hair, and her face was thin. She wore red lipstick and often smiled gently as she spoke.

"Were you one of the little boys I used to see in your neighborhood?" she asked. "I remember one little boy came along once on his three-wheeler and said to me, 'Your dress is pretty.' Years later I was wearing the same dress and that boy—of course, he was older by then—came up to me again and said, 'I like your dress.'"

I remembered, as a boy, once saying hi to Grace. Maybe I'd also said something about her dress. I couldn't remember, but I hoped I had said it.

That morning in the apartment, Grace had on a simple black housedress; as we spoke, her gnarled fingers played at the large buttons up the front. She wore flat shoes and thick, tan stockings rolled below the knee.

Which house on Sandringham did I live in? Grace asked. I said I lived about halfway down the street where two split-level ranch houses with circular driveways sat side by side. They looked so similar in design, and both were fronted in light-colored brick, that visitors often confused them until I had the brick on mine painted over in a taupe color.

"Oh, yes," she said. "I know those two houses. I like the other one better. I could never understand why you'd paint over the brick."

Grace said she began walking in the summer of 1960, a fact I seized on for a theory as to why she had started walking in the first place: in 1955, after Dwight Eisenhower's heart attack, his personal physician, Dr. Paul Dudley White, had urged Americans to get more exercise, such as biking and brisk walks. Wasn't that why Grace had started walking?

"No," she said, "I didn't walk for exercise. I did it more to let off steam, sort of. I guess I just had energy to work off. It became a compulsion, really."

Grace Field was born in Binghamton, New York, in 1914. Later, she and her family moved to Rochester, where her father ran a successful photo supply business. She grew up in a city neighborhood until age fourteen, when the family moved to Brighton. At the Eastman School of Music in Rochester she studied harp and piano, and then, in her twenties, moved to Manhattan to study harp at the Julliard School. From a box of old papers, she pulled out a card with the photo of a young, attractive, dark-haired woman. "Miss Grace Field, Harp and Celtic Harp, Available for Solo & Ensemble Work, Churches– Clubs–Private Gatherings." It listed a phone number and address on Manhattan's East Side.

"I just sold it a couple of years ago," Grace said when I asked if she still had a harp. She said she couldn't find any new music and got bored playing the same pieces over and over again. Same thing with her piano. She sold that, too.

Against the wall near where we were seated was a long wooden table where the piano had been. The table was covered with spoons, and also with angel figurines, and tiny harps carved from wood.

When she lived in New York City, Grace had a boyfriend, a young man who had wanted to study Irish harp. Later, he asked her to marry him, but she declined his proposal when she learned that his ninety-year-old mother would have to live with them.

Since then, Grace had lived alone. "I'm just an old maid," she said with a sad laugh.

After eighteen years in New York, Grace returned to Rochester, took a job at the library, and moved into a modest home on a little street in Brighton called School House Lane.

She chose Sandringham and nearby streets to walk on because of their beauty. "I admired the homes, and it's also shady," she explained. "The heat bothers me. But in your neighborhood I can almost walk the whole way in the shade." The trees along Sandringham form a canopy over the sidewalk that offers nearly continuous shade. In a light rain, you could walk a good part of the way without even getting wet.

Grace would drive to a corner near Sandringham, then walk up and down the street and around the neighborhood for about a half an hour. At a brisk pace of about four miles an hour, she'd cover about two miles.

"I saw all kinds of things," she said, remembering some of the highlights of her years of walking. She remembers the time in the 1960s when a judge's house at the corner of Sandringham was bombed, and when people marched outside the home of a doctor who did abortions with signs that said, THIS MAN MURDERS BABIES.

And she remembers the murder-suicide at the Willses' house. "I heard it on the news and I thought, 'Oh, my. I pass that house all the time.' I believe the house was empty for a while after that."

In four decades of walking, had she gotten to know many of the people who live on Sandringham?

"No, not many," she said. "In the early days I made a friendly acquaintance with one couple, but then they died off and the new generation are not so interested in knowing an old lady."

She added, "There is a doctor who lives over there near you. I believe his name is Guzzetta. I became acquainted with him walking his dog, Heidi. I have a niece also named Heidi. He's a nice man. He lost his wife a few years back.

"I also became acquainted with the mailman," she continued. "One day I dropped my purse getting out of my car and the mailman—he was new at the time—picked it up for me."

I wanted to know what Grace meant when she said the reason she walked was to "let off steam."

What did she think about while she walked?

"A lot of time I was just admiring the homes," she said. "Or sometimes I'd play games with myself, like counting trees, counting how many steps I'd take in a minute, or counting the number of steps between lampposts. I used to apply music to my walking, too. I used to walk in different time signatures."

I asked Grace to show me how she walked in time signatures. She got up and in slow, careful steps made her way across the beige-carpeted floor to an open area in the middle of the room. Then she demonstrated how she would walk in 2/4 time—a straightforward stride toward the door, one foot and then the other; then 3/4 time—a kind of forward waltz back to me.

"I'd walk in triplets, too," she said, and she moved toward the door in a kind of stuttering step, her right foot moving out to the side with accents on alternating feet.

"I remember that!" I nearly shouted, suddenly recalling as a boy seeing her walk in front of my house with that unusual step.

Grace was limping again and returned to her chair.

When I asked how she coped with loneliness, Grace answered, "I have some good memories," and mentioned, as an example, a time in New York City when she drove with friends across the Brooklyn Bridge in an open convertible, holding her harp in the backseat. "People were shouting and waving at us," she recalled, smiling.

What would she miss if she had to give up walking? I asked.

"I'd miss walking," she said, "and the beauty of your neighborhood."

I wondered if Grace had ever wished that she herself had lived on Sandringham. "No," she said without hesitation. "I liked my little house with my parents, and then my other little house on School House Lane. I knew all my neighbors. Every time someone moved in, they'd have a big party to welcome them. Your neighborhood is lovely, but I never see people in their front yards, and they don't have front porches. When I was young, everyone would sit out on their porches and people would walk by and visit."

WHEN I said good-bye to Grace, we hugged at her apartment door. As I held her, I was surprised just how little there was of her.

It made me sad to think that Grace Field had walked through my neighborhood nearly every day for more than forty years, counting lampposts and walking in triplets, yet aside from perhaps one couple who had long since passed on, none of us had gotten to know her. Put another way: Grace had, in effect, invited all of us to be her neighbor, but none of us had. Maybe she could have given some child on our street piano or harp lessons, or taught us how to keep fit long before it was fashionable. None of that happened, though, and now it was very close to too late.

Whether I said "Hi" one day and complimented Grace Field on her dress or not, still I had grown up on that street and mostly ignored her. Even as an adult, I ignored her. I saw Grace. I spoke about her. But I didn't speak to her.

If Renan Wills and her family had left a light footprint in our neighborhood, then Grace Field, despite having walked past our homes day after day for more than forty years—that's nearly fifteen thousand times—had left virtually no footprint, until now.

My thank-you note to Grace for letting me visit, and her note to me, crossed in the mail. Her card, with yellow butterflies on the front, thanked me for coming over to talk with her. She enclosed a gift: a cloth bookmark she'd woven by hand, an intricate design in brown and white.

I wish we'd better woven Grace into our neighborhood when we had the chance.

4

The Top of Their Games

ON the same day Bob Wills shot his wife and himself, a young Rochester couple, vacationing in the Cayman Islands, made an offer to buy a house on Sandringham Road. "I called my sister the next day to tell her we'd faxed in the offer," recalled Deb O'Dell. "That's when she gave us the news. Later, when we were back in town and told people we were moving to Sandringham, they all said, 'Oh, are you buying *that* house?' They thought we were buying the Willses' house. It didn't bother us, though."

The house that Deb and Dave O'Dell bought is the house next to mine, on the other side of me from Lou Guzzetta. At the time I approached them, the O'Dells had been married just four years, and Deb, thirty-two, was Sandringham's youngest homeowner.

My contact with the O'Dells, since they had moved in about a year earlier, had been brief but pleasant. They did some of their own yard work, and on nice days when we both happened to be outside, we would sometimes chat over the fence. So calling Deb on a Sunday to see if I could stop by to talk about a "new writing project," as I termed it, was not difficult. She invited me over that same afternoon.

THE O'Dells' home, built in 1937, was one of the stately older houses on the street. Constructed of red brick, it was modeled after French country estates. It had a steeply pitched, pavilion roof covered in slate shingles. The interior featured hardwood floors and French doors. My house, in comparison—with its ranch-style horizontal lines and plain brick façade—seemed bland.

At 4 p.m., I walked next door to visit with Deb. She welcomed me in and showed me to the kitchen, where we sat at the breakfast table. Deb was petite, with shoulder-length brown hair and a wholesome look. Nearby, a beautifully groomed golden retriever—named Cayman, after the island where Deb and Dave vacation—was eager to play. I'm writing a book about how people live as neighbors, I told Deb, as I gave her a hardcover copy of my previous book. I asked about her experience since moving into her new home. She said things had mostly gone well. She said she hadn't met many of the neighbors and would like to, but on the other hand, she and Dave didn't have a lot of free time. They were both kept busy with work—each had an active career in business—decorating the house, and sports. In the winters they played volleyball and paddle tennis, and in the summers, Deb enjoyed golf at the country club. As well, they each had family in town. In the warmer months, they liked to be away every weekend at a Finger Lakes cottage about thirty miles south of Rochester owned by Dave's family.

I asked Deb if she'd be willing to talk with me, let me get to know her by hanging around on a typical day, and to write about it. I didn't mention the sleeping over part; it would sound too weird coming right at the start. Deb seemed interested and said she'd talk it over with Dave, who was out of town on business, and call me back in a few days.

A full week passed and I didn't hear from her, so I called back. Deb asked if I could come over again—when Dave would be home—to meet with them both together.

My son once described Dave O'Dell as looking like the actor Robert Redford, and later, when I mentioned it to Dave, he said he'd been told that before. He was a large man—6 foot 4 inches, 220 pounds—a full foot taller than his wife. Dave had a ruddy face, strong jaw, and hair so blond it was nearly luminous. The three of us—Dave, Deb, and I—sat around the kitchen table. I repeated my proposal and emphasized again, as I had earlier with Deb, that I'd already interviewed and spent considerable time with Lou Guzzetta. That seemed to reassure Dave, and prompted him to tell a story about his one encounter with Lou. "It was about a year after we'd moved in," Dave began in his strong, deep voice, "and I'm washing windows on the front of the house. I'm up there on the ladder with my back to the street and I hear this big, booming voice behind me: 'Please! You shouldn't be doing that. You're crazy!' I look down and it's this older guy. 'You gotta let a professional do that,' he says. 'One slip, one fall, and your whole life is over!'"

So did Dave still wash the windows himself?

"Sure I do," he said with a big laugh. "But now, every time I get on the ladder, I think, 'Can I do this without Dr. Guzzetta seeing me?'"

Over the course of several weeks, I talked with Deb and Dave together—even watched them one evening play in their weekly co-ed volleyball league—as well as separately. Deb agreed to let me spend all of an upcoming Monday with her, and then, on the Sunday afternoon before, she and Dave agreed that I could sleep over that night.

A few hours later, I was sitting on a four-poster pine bed in an upstairs guest room in the O'Dells' house. Deb had welcomed me in, showed me to the room, and invited me to get settled while she finished some laundry, and to come downstairs when I was ready. I hung a clean shirt in the closet, for the next day. There was a wetsuit hanging—must be what Dave wore, I guessed, when he went scuba diving in the Cayman Islands. The room was done up in early American style: blue-and-white-pinstriped wallpaper, yellow-and-blue curtains; a medallion on the side of the bed said the bed was a "reproduction certified by the Museum of American Folk Art." Very classy; nothing like that in my house.

Actually, I could hardly believe I was even in that house, let alone as an invited guest. To me, as a child, the people who then lived there—my family's next-door neighbors—seemed unfriendly, even scary. They had a blind dog, a deaf housekeeper, and they might all have been mute, as far as I was concerned, because I can't remember a single word any of them—parents or children—ever spoke to me. Retrieving a basketball from their front yard was only a little less frightening than running up to touch Boo Radley's front porch.

Years later, when I asked my dad what was going on between us and the Prewitts—I'm changing their name here—he gave a couple of different explanations. One was that when he built our house, to meet the town code, he had to raise the level of our backyard a few feet. "We had to bring all this dirt over to cover the basement," he told me, "but it also covered their fence. Apparently, they had not conformed to the regulations. That was the first falling-out we had with them." This part, evidently, was accurate because even today some sections of the metal fence that runs between my backyard and the O'Dells' were less than two feet high—the rest was buried. But at other times my dad suggested that the Prewitts were just not thrilled to have us move in next to them. Whether this was true or not, I didn't know. "She was a society matron," my dad said, speaking of Mrs. Prewitt. "Every year over there, she'd have her Vassar Club luncheon." My dad grew up poor and couldn't afford to go to college. "They lived in a different world," he continued. "We didn't bother with them and they didn't bother with us."

A twist to this story is that, after my parents and the Prewitts retired, they both, by chance, moved to the same apartment building. One day I went over to visit my parents, and when the lobby elevator door opened, there standing inside were my dad and Mr. Prewitt—he was steadying himself with a cane—both in their eighties, riding side by side in silence. Neighbors, one might say, to the end.

And there I was, on a Sunday evening, a guest in the Prewitts' former home, resting on a four-poster bed.

Downstairs, I found Dave in the family room at the back of the house watching TV while he and Cayman played tug-of-war with a knotted rope toy. He wore jeans and a CAYMAN ISLANDS T-shirt. Soon Deb appeared holding a pile of folded laundry, which she was going to put away upstairs. A few minutes later, she returned in sweat clothes, ready for a workout in the basement gym.

In the family room, Dave and I watched some more TV, mostly without talking. He sat in a big, leather easy chair. When Deb came up from the basement, we all watched a little of the eleven o'clock news, then climbed the winding staircase together—Deb, Dave, Cayman, and I. On the way up, Dave warned me about the alarm system.

"Whatever you do," he said in his deep voice, "don't go downstairs in the morning until we turn the alarm off. It's got a motion detector and it's really loud; you don't want to hear it."

"Yeah," agreed Deb. "You don't want to hear it. It's ugly."

At the top of the stairs, we said good night. They turned left into the master bedroom, along with Cayman. I turned right into the guest room, then went to a bathroom down the hall to wash up.

The bathroom was probably original with the house: the shower stall and tub were made of thick white marble. The wallpaper had a circus motif: pen-and-ink drawings of acrobats, clowns, a circus train, and elephants marching in a row connected trunk to tail. I could imagine a child brushing his teeth there, losing himself in the intricacy of that circus design, and wondered if the wallpaper went all the way back to the Prewitts.

I unpacked. If it hadn't been so late, I might have called my parents, just for the fun of telling them I was sleeping overnight in a guest room in the Prewitts' house.

"DAVE? Dave?" I called in a stage whisper, leaning over the wooden banister. There was no response. It was quarter past six on Monday morning and I was on the upstairs landing of the O'Dells' house. I got up at 5:30 because Dave told me he gets up at six and I wanted to be ready to see him when he came out of his bedroom. The problem was the door to Dave and Deb's room was closed but I didn't know if he was still in there or if, while I was shaving, he had already gone downstairs. But I couldn't go down to check because if he hadn't gone down yet, I'd trip the alarm. I imagined something like those deep blasts from fire trucks followed by Dave and Deb rushing from the bedroom in pajamas, with Cayman in pursuit barking and snapping at me.

That would not be a good way to start the day.

I heard a noise, but I couldn't tell if it was coming from inside Deb and Dave's room or from downstairs.

"Dave?" I whispered again.

There was nothing to do but wait.

As I did, I found myself contrasting my experiences with the O'Dells and with Lou. For sure, they had welcomed me, but the bond I felt wasn't as immediate as the one I'd had with Lou. And I didn't sense that the O'Dells, at least at that point in their lives, needed a sense of community to the extent I did. After all, Deb and Dave were young and recently married, and led full, busy lives that were largely self-contained. Deb didn't need the YMCA, as Lou did; she had her own workout room in the basement. Dave didn't need neighbors to help him care for his property; healthy and vigorous, he could handle much of the home maintenance. Their family room was an entertainment center, complete with a large TV. They didn't need a neighborhood park; their backyard was large and beautifully landscaped. To look at their hectic schedules, it was a wonder they'd even been able to fit me in for the sleepover. Yet maybe the O'Dells were more typical than Lou of the way many people actually live as neighbors today.

Finally, at 6:30 a.m., Dave strode out of the bedroom, his hair still wet from the shower. For his job as vice-president of sales and marketing for a Rochester firm that made PC-based cash registers, he wore a button-down shirt, khaki pants, and brown tassel loafers.

"Good morning," Dave said matter-of-factly, as if seeing me outside his bedroom door first thing in the morning were a regular occurrence. He hurried downstairs with the dog, calling over his shoulder, "I've gotta take Cayman out to the bathroom!" Half a minute later, he was back with the morning paper. He wiped his feet, wiped Cayman's feet, and then filled Cayman's food bowl. Dave was gentle and attentive with Cayman; it was easy to imagine he'd be good with kids.

In the kitchen, Dave grabbed a doughnut and a can of Mountain Dew. He said it was his regular breakfast. He stuffed the soda in a pocket of his black leather jacket, wished me a good day, and left the house. As he backed quickly out of the driveway in his Ford SUV, I checked my watch: it'd been just seven minutes since he came out of the bedroom.

I waited in the kitchen for Deb to come down. On the table stood a greeting card. The outside read: "For the Beautiful Woman Who Shares My Life." It was a Valentine from Dave, still displayed nearly a month after the holiday. Deb and Dave would soon celebrate their fifth anniversary. They had met while both were working at Bausch & Lomb, the eye-care company headquartered in Rochester. Deb was in finance and Dave was in sales. Less than two years after they started dating, Dave proposed one summer evening on the upper deck of a Finger Lakes dinner-cruise ship.

I heard Deb starting down the stairs.

"Good morning!" she said brightly, stepping into the kitchen dressed in a cotton sweater and khakis.

Deb prepared breakfast—toasted bagels with cream cheese, banana slices, and tea—and we watched the morning news on a countertop TV. We didn't know each other well enough to express political views, so neither of us commented.

The phone rang. "You're up early," said Deb. It was her sister, Carol. Deb asked, "Do you want to have dinner over here before paddle?" She meant before their paddle tennis match that evening. She and her sister played as partners in a women's league and they had a game scheduled that evening at the Country Club of Rochester, which is just around the corner from Sandringham Road.

While drinking tea, Deb reviewed papers for work. She was recently hired to set up and manage a local office for a Boston-based consulting firm, and she was expecting, sometime early this morning, a call from her boss. The downtown office Deb had rented for the firm wasn't ready yet, so she still worked at home.

Done with breakfast, she went upstairs to her second-floor study, a small room with desks on either end—one for her and one for Dave. I sat at Dave's desk and swiveled around to watch Deb work. Her manicured nails clicked rapidly across the keyboard as she logged on to the desktop computer and filled in last week's time sheet. Typically, Deb worked nine to ten hours a day, but often much longer when her boss visited in town or she had other meetings. "I love what I do," she told me. There were days, she confessed, when if Dave wasn't home, she might work all night. As it was, she often slept just six hours. "I can be up till midnight working on a business plan for a client," she said, "then up at five thirty, and on the computer by six thirty or seven, e-mailing stuff for clients. Honestly, even walking the dog is frustrating sometimes because I have to stop working."

When away from work, Deb often got "itchy." In the Cayman Islands, she said, "After five days, I'm ready to come home. I go nutty. Dave could stay longer. His parents stay a month and we get along great, but there's nothing to do. His family competes to see who reads the most books." On their last trip, Dave read three spy thrillers; Deb read half of a book on high-tech marketing.

Just then, Cayman came into the study with the bristle end of my toothbrush sticking out of his mouth. I'd forgotten that earlier that morning I'd left it on top of my suitcase, intending to brush after breakfast. Good-naturedly, Deb asked if I would like to brush now.

While she waited for her boss to call, Deb e-mailed clients and colleagues.

Moments later, the phone rang.

"Hello!" said Deb with a broad smile. It was her boss. She brought a large sheet of lined paper—her to-do list—to the top of a pile of memos, notes, and proposals.

"I just got a call from that gene therapy guy," Deb told her boss. "I submitted the proposal to him last Friday."

The "gene therapy guy" was a local cancer researcher. Deb's firm provided business advice to start-up companies, most of them in biosciences and information technology, and this new local company would be a good client.

"Do you want me to do anything there?" she asked her boss. "Sure, I'll take the number if you have it."

Deb displayed an impressive self-confidence to let me listen in on her business calls. I was amazed how focused she could be with an observer in the room, especially one scratching notes in a reporter's notebook.

*　　*　　*

DEB O'Dell grew up in Fulton, New York, a small town north of Syracuse. Her father, though he never went to college, rose to become head of financial services for the town's biggest employer, Nestlé Company. "So we always had chocolate in the house," Deb recalled earlier. From an early age she knew she wanted a career in business. "When I was young," she recalled, "Dad and I talked sports, and then as I got older, we talked business. He was my inspiration."

Deb remembered her small-town neighborhood fondly. "Growing up, we had great relationships with our neighbors," she said, "people borrowing things, helping each other out." Deb's mother, a retired school teacher, still lived in Fulton. "Since Dad died," Deb told me, "Mom's one of three widows on the street, and they all look out for each other." She said one of the other women lives right across the street and she and her mom have a system where when they wake up in the morning, they raise their window shades so they each know the other is okay. "And if someone comes to her house and Mom's not sure who it is," said Deb, "she'll call the lady across the street to see if she can identify the person."

Deb's father died when Deb was still in her twenties, but given her rapid rise after college as a business analyst, he at least lived to see the beginnings of his daughter's successful career.

ON the phone, Deb and her boss moved quickly from one business topic to another. In her right hand, she twirled a pink ballpoint pen between two manicured fingers. The effect was of a teenager wrapped around the phone, lost in the emotional intensity of the call.

"Yup, yup . . . yup," she said. "Okay. Yup . . . all right. I have a feeling this is going to be a big meeting, just a brain dump on these people."

"Okay, we're going to continue later this afternoon, right? Great!"

Deb hung up and straightened herself in the chair. "My to-do list is getting doubled after that call," she said with mock complaint.

After hardly a minute's break, she called a prospect in Buffalo.

Then her cell phone rang.

"Hello, this is Deb."

AT 10:30, there was a momentary lull in Deb's phone traffic.

"You know," I said, "with reasonable certainty, I think I can tell you where Lou Guzzetta is and what he's doing at this exact moment."

I had remembered that 10:30 is when Lou took his morning nap. I was curious how Deb would respond, whether she'd find my reference to our neighbor to be of any interest.

"Really?" she asked. "So what do you think he's doing right now?"

"Well, I think he's in a cozy room—he calls it 'the library'— at the front of his house," I said, "lying on his back on a black leather sofa, taking a nap. There's a program of international news on the TV, but he's not listening, and Heidi, his schnauzer, is sitting on a leather armchair in the corner."

"I know that dog," said Deb. "I've seen him in the window barking when I walk by."

For a moment, I felt a calm overtake Deb's study.

"So how do you know all that about Lou?" she asked.

I reminded her I'd spent a day with Lou inside his house, just as I'm doing now with her.

After a pause, she said, "That's so cool that you know that."

Then her cell phone rang.

"Hello, this is Deb."

The call was brief. Afterward, I asked why she said it was cool to know that Lou was napping.

"I don't know," she said. "As I walk by all these houses, I sometimes wonder what's going on in them. I guess that he was taking a nap just shows all the things we have in common—I mean, everybody naps sometimes—but it also shows how different we are 'cause I would never nap at ten thirty in the morning."

I sensed in Deb a real attraction to the idea of making a connection with Lou, but also a wariness, like even if the connection were made, she wouldn't quite know what to do with it, or have the time to pursue it.

"Getting back to Lou," she said, "of course, what you're getting in all the different houses on the street is just a snapshot in time. Things could look different a year or two from now."

That sounded like an opening into what could be another topic, something I'd wanted to ask Deb about.

"Do you mean people could be doing different things in a year?" I asked.

"Right," she said.

"Like their families could change?"

"Yeah," she said.

"Are you and Dave trying to have a family now?" I sensed, even as I said it, that without the sleepover we never would have achieved the intimacy that would allow me to ask the question.

"We're in that mode," she said. "We've been trying for about two years. Of course, you've seen our schedules. It's not like we're really focused on making this happen."

"You mean with work and sports and everything?" I asked.

"Right. Anyway, it'd be impossible to do this if I had kids," she said, motioning toward the stack of papers on her desk. "I just couldn't do it. It's bad enough with the dog."

The previous week, I'd gone food shopping with Deb and watched as she pushed her cart rapidly through the store, tossing in packages of meat, declaring halfheartedly after each one, "That's a meal." She threw in a few other items, including frozen bagels, Doritos, and a twelve-pack of Mountain Dew, until the cart was half-full. We were in and out of the store in half an hour. "It's scary to compare my shopping cart with Carol's," she'd said, referring to how long it takes her sister, who has two young children, to shop.

Earlier, I'd talked to Dave about his hopes for starting a family. "We have five bedrooms and we'd love to fill them," said Dave, who is forty-two, ten years older than Deb. "I look at people who have children and I get envious. Friends from high school bring their kids to our cottage at the lake. Some of the kids are ten already. Some are teenagers. It amazes me. I always thought I'd be married young and be a young dad active with my kids."

Back in the study, Deb's cell phone rang.

"Hello, this is Deb."

Later, Deb called her boss back, her third call to him in two hours.

"Hello!" she said. "Hey, the guy called me back on that contract. All righty. That's it. I gotta get going to pick up lunch. I've got a meeting at the new office."

* * *

DEB and I drove in her Saab to the downtown office she'd rented for her firm so she could meet over lunch with a prospective employee. Once there, Deb excused herself to a conference room, and I had a look around the office.

Deb had picked a first-class location. In a few more weeks, she would vacate her upstairs study on Sandringham and instead sit at a big desk in this penthouse suite, the downtown skyline behind her, managing perhaps half a dozen employees—many of them older than she. My young neighbor was an impressive businesswoman.

As we drove home, Deb told me she'd already decided against hiring the applicant she'd just met with—in Deb's opinion, she didn't have the social skills needed for the job.

BACK at the house, Deb changed into jeans and a sweater; there were no more business meetings scheduled that day. She then went straight to the study to prepare for a 2:30 conference call. I was impressed: she hadn't taken a break since she started that morning at seven. Nearly two hours later, she was still in the study, juggling calls on both lines. Around five, she said she needed to take Cayman out for a walk and invited me to join her. "Do you like this purple sweater with the jeans?" she asked. "Doesn't go, does it?" I told her the sweater looked fine, but she changed into a brown one anyway.

Deb walked with Cayman on a leash. As we passed Lou's house, I saw a light in the kitchen and figured Lou was either preparing dinner or else still in the living room on the sofa with a tumbler of gin, watching the closing stock report.

As we walked, I pointed to houses on both sides of Sandringham and asked Deb if she knew the people who lived there. "No, no clue, nope," she responded. She said she did recognize a few residents as members of her country club, but as for the rest she had no relationships with any of them "other than waving," as she put it.

She seemed frustrated not to have made those connections. Did she meet people while walking the dog?

"You can have a brief conversation with people," she said, "but then you notice that it's the same conversation ten times. And then there's the thing where people introduce their dogs and not themselves! What's with that? And the really irritating thing," she continued, grimacing, "is that I've started doing it myself."

She said that when she and Dave moved in, they had planned to invite the immediate neighbors over for a little party, but when they got to know the neighborhood better, they felt a party would be out of place. "Those kinds of things just aren't done," she said. "Dave and I haven't been invited to a single party."

That's a failing of this neighborhood, I thought. It was nice of Deb and Dave even to consider having a party to meet the neighborhood, but in many neighborhoods, it works the other way: longtime neighbors throw a party to meet the new people.

Cayman stopped to sniff at a fire hydrant.

"Where I grew up," continued Deb, "people borrowed stuff and helped each other. But here—the other night, I needed vanilla for cookies and I made Dave drive to the store in a snowstorm to get it."

Why hadn't she just asked her next-door neighbor—me—for vanilla?

"It just doesn't seem like people do that here," she said.

Deb said she used to ask neighbors to watch the house when she and Dave went out of town. "But then we realized they really didn't care," she said.

How could she tell?

"You could just tell," she said. "That's okay, though. I know people are busy. Dave and I sure are." Now, when she and Dave go away—including nearly every summer weekend—Deb asks her sister, fifteen minutes away, to check on the house.

"The thing is," she said, "the people on this street, I don't think they want to know you."

DEB was on to something. As I later learned, this street might actually have been designed for people who don't want to know each other. Sandringham Road—and the subdivision it is part of—was built in the 1920s by Houston Barnard, the highly successful engineer and developer.

Barnard, born in 1871, was named after his maternal grandfather, Isaac Houston, who ran a prosperous tavern and stagecoach stop between Rochester and Buffalo. Houston Barnard grew up in relative comfort, studied civil engineering, and by age twenty-one was chief engineer of a railway company. Later, through his own firm, he received contracts for some of the largest public works projects of the time: the first tunnel under the Hudson River, reclamation of Boston's Back Bay, and reconstruction of sections of the Erie Canal. Barnard gained a listing in the social registry and joined Rochester's most exclusive country club. During World War I, he donated his private yacht to the U.S. government for use as a cruiser. In a photo taken in his prime, Barnard, a man of ample girth in a white summer suit and horn-rim glasses, appears healthy, content, and confident.

Around 1918, Barnard began work on his "crown jewel," the upscale neighborhood that would bear his name, and include my family's home. On 116 acres of what had been mostly apple and pear orchards, he laid out three roads, each 30 feet wide. Speaking of similar suburban roads, Kenneth Jackson, in his book *Crabgrass Frontier*, explains, "The width of the street was not necessitated by heavy vehicular traffic but rather by the ideal of spaciousness itself." Barnard provided sidewalks and street-lights, and planted each side of the street with an alternating pattern of European lindens and Douglas firs. And he wrote a code to ensure that only the finest homes would grace his streets: minimum frontage would be at least 75 feet, the main wall could be no nearer than 50 feet from the street, and no house could be nearer than 10 feet from the side lot line.

Of the three streets Barnard laid out, the middle one would be the most graceful. From its southern end, it would climb a moderate slope northward, curve gently to the right, and descend gradually to its eastern end point. Barnard called this half-mile-long, crescent-shaped street Cherry Road.

For a while, it all worked. European-trained architects designed some grand houses for wealthy clients, mostly Anglo-American, English, and French period homes in the popular Colonial, Tudor, and Chateauesque Revival styles. But sales were slower than expected. Barnard tried what today would be called rebranding, renaming the streets to give them a more distinguished tone. Orchard Road became Ambassador, Morris Road became Esplanade, and Cherry Road, that wide, central boulevard with the gentle northeasterly curve he renamed after the private country estate of the Queen of England: Sandringham.

Then the stock market crashed. By 1930, only ten homes had been built on Sandringham; twice that many lots remained vacant. A few more houses would go up between then and the post–World War II boom, but not enough to save Houston Barnard from bankruptcy. Soon after, he fell ill. In an attempt to regain his health, Barnard sailed to the Mediterranean, but in 1936, at age sixty-five, he died in Nice, France.

Houston Barnard's wife had passed away before he did; there were no children. His body was returned to Rochester.

To my mind, from the way Barnard designed the neighborhood—wide streets, broad lots, deep setbacks—he didn't expect neighbors to have much connection with each other. Indeed, most of the people who chose to live there probably didn't need connections, either. As the advertisement said, this was meant to be a neighborhood of "high character," meaning it was for people of wealth and social status.

Yet I wonder, if Houston Barnard had built Sandringham Road later in his life—not when he was at the top of his game, but when he was bankrupt, sick, and alone—if he might have designed the street differently. Maybe he would have planned for some common space, just half a lot reserved as a tiny park where he himself could have sat on a warm afternoon. There he might have met a neighbor to sit with and talk. Maybe after enough friendly chats, Barnard would have felt safe enough to tell his neighbor how he was feeling; how lonely he was since his wife died, perhaps that he regretted not having children, or how humiliated he felt to be bankrupt, and how it felt to be ill. Maybe he would have then gone home, relieved—at least for that one day—by having unburdened himself and fostered a momentary connection, however small.

"HELLO, this is Deb." Just as Deb and I returned to the house at about six o'clock, her boss called. She would be going to Boston later that week for a business meeting, and he wanted her to stop in Albany on the way to meet with state officials.

Then Dave called to say he'd be home in half an hour and to start dinner without him.

Deb's sister, Carol, with whom Deb would play as partners in a paddle tennis match after dinner, was already at the house. The three of us ate while watching the evening news.

When Dave arrived, after some roughhousing with Cayman and a kiss hello for both Deb and Carol, he said kindly, "Deborah, you're going to be late."

Deb and Carol and I put our coats on and headed toward the door.

"It's the last match of the season, girls," Dave reminded them. "I expect you to win it. Good luck!"

Deb and I rode together to the country club in her Saab; Carol, who would go home after the game, drove separately. But as soon as I closed the car door, even before we backed out of the driveway, Deb turned to me.

"If you must know," she said, "this weekend I had a meltdown."

I hadn't asked about the weekend, so her confession took me by surprise.

"I fell apart," she said. "It was a crazy, busy week. My to-do list was long. I was sick and didn't feel well enough to go out at night. I can get frustrated when things get too overwhelming. I started getting upset and asking Dave, 'Why am I doing this job? Why this, why that?' Eventually, I was raging, frustrated with everything, even Cayman. I yelled, 'I don't feel well! Why do I have to play with the dog?' and then the dog swings this knotted rope and it hits me in the neck—I mean really hard. It left a mark, and that kind of got me out of the rage."

I asked how Dave responded to her "meltdown."

"He's helpful by not overreacting," she said.

I wasn't sure what had triggered Deb's confession; maybe it was the intimacy created by us being together all day, or just by getting into the car together. I was glad she felt close enough to confide in me, though, and I wondered, as we drove, if I had not met Deb and we'd not gotten to know each other so quickly because of the sleepover, to whom she might have unloaded. Maybe even for a generally happy, busy, and successful young person, it's nice to have a neighbor nearby to vent to once in a while.

IT was fifteen degrees with a steady, light snow when Deb and I arrived at the country club for paddle tennis. The game, which is also called "platform tennis," is played much like regular tennis but on a smaller court, with shorter rackets and a rubber ball. When one of the women on the opposing team called to say she would be late, Deb asked if I would like to play. I'd never played paddle tennis, but it looked like fun and I could use the exercise; I'd been sitting much of the day.

"Sure, I'll play," I said, putting down my notebook and pen.

My teammate, a woman about Deb's age, and I won the first two games, but in the end Deb and Carol beat us six games to three. Then the missing player showed up.

After a quick warm-up for the new player, the competition began. At the net, Deb assumed an aggressive stance: knees flexed, two hands holding the racket straight out in front of her, ready to block any return. Waiting for the serve, she squatted to stretch, rose at the hips, then straightened her back. She flipped her paddle over, crouched, swayed left and then right, exhaled visible breath into the night air. Then she attacked the ball.

Her return lifted the ball over the server's head and to the far side of the court, just inside the double foul line.

Compared to the other women on the court, Deb was quicker and more intense. The others also crouched to receive a serve, but their crouching was studied; hers was instinctive. She dominated the game. The others played; Deb competed.

As I watched Deb on the court, I understood that at that point in her life, her business and social calendars were happily full. Even though she remembered warmly the close, small-town neighborhood she grew up in, her need for connections with neighbors now was only modest. Maybe later, when life settled down, there'd be more time for neighborly connections.

In the meantime, as Deb moved crosscourt for a killer overhead shot, I hoped the next time she needed vanilla, she would think to come over and borrow some.

5

No Bed, No Breakfast

WHEN Lou Guzzetta approached me on the sidewalk, I was surprised and concerned to see a cast on his right arm. He was walking Heidi—holding her leash in his left hand—and I was walking my dog, Champ. Before I could ask Lou about the cast, though, he razzed me. "Get that mongrel out of the neighborhood!" he shouted. We'd adopted Champ, as Lou well knew, from the animal shelter, and he was an unusual mix of black Lab and dachshund—he had the large head and tail of a Lab but stood only eleven inches high. "This neighborhood is for purebreds! Does that dog have papers and a proper pedigree?"

The thing about Champ was, even though he was small, he had a strong personality; among neighborhood dogs, he was the alpha male. If he were a person, he might have been a surgeon. Lou seemed to understand this, and though he teased me about Champ, I think he respected him.

I asked Lou about his arm. He said he had been in Virginia

the previous weekend visiting his daughter when he tripped at night on a curb. "I fell straight out on the pavement," he said. The fall broke two bones in his right hand and wrist and, as he put it, "took the skin of both legs from the knees to the ankles." I asked Lou if there was anything he needed help with around the house, but he said he was handling things okay and expected to get the cast off soon. He said he missed his exercise class at the Y. "Without me, those guys are all desperate," he said, referring to his buddies there. "I get calls, 'When are you coming back?' 'Hey, everything's dead here without you.'"

It worried me that Lou had fallen. I thought he was lucky that all he broke was his hand and wrist. What if he'd broken a hip? Who would take care of him?

FOLLOWING my sleepovers at Lou's and at the O'Dells', I decided that—for variety's sake—I would like to try sleeping over at a household with children. In the directory put out by the neighborhood association, some families listed their children's ages, so I could tell who had children living at home. I began approaching each one, but soon discovered I was striking out. Perhaps I shouldn't have been surprised, but Lou and Dave and Deb had welcomed me so warmly, and the sleepovers had gone so well, that when the other neighbors said no, the rejections stung.

The first couple I tried—they had three children at home—were a forty-five-year-old research scientist and her husband, an architect. She was rumored to be nearing an important breakthrough in biomedicine. I called ahead and on a Sunday afternoon walked over to their home to explain what I wanted to do. They said no, explaining that her work was too sensitive to risk being revealed prematurely in a book. I offered to omit any mention of the specifics of her work, but they still said no. "Maybe when I retire," she said, "if you're still working on the book, we can talk again."

Right.

My next pick was a couple—he a stockbroker and she a homemaker—with two teenage children. I knew him to say hello to, but was unsure how to make the approach. Late one afternoon, I was walking Champ past his house just as he happened to pull into his driveway, and decided to speak to him right there. I briefly described what I had in mind and said, if he was interested, we could have lunch to discuss it further. With a grave look on his face, he came close to me, poked his cell phone at my chest, and said in a low, controlled voice, "I'm a very private person. In fact, you might say I am pathologically private. I wouldn't ever want to see anything in print about me, my family, or my business." I was wondering if I should take that as a no when, oddly, he said he'd be glad to have lunch. We set a date, but later he canceled. We rescheduled, and he canceled again. Then one morning he called and invited me to his house. He let me interview him for an hour about his personal background, which turned out to be fascinating. But a few weeks later, just before our next scheduled meeting, he called to say he couldn't do it—he was just "too private a person."

The third refusal came from a couple with four children who recently had emigrated from Eastern Europe. When I visited at their home to talk, they served tea and homemade pastries. The mother and father each had a compelling personal story, but they ultimately declined to participate. Exposure of their family backgrounds, they said, might jeopardize relatives left behind.

So my success rate with the neighbors had dropped quite low

(two yeses and four nos, including the one neighbor before Lou who turned me down). But then I thought of Jamie Columbus.

I knew Jamie, at least a little. In fact, if there was one person on my street whom most people knew—or at least knew of—it was Jamie Columbus. She, along with her mother, was among the most active real estate agents in town, and her specialty was buying and selling homes in the Houston Barnard neighborhood. In fact, after Renan Wills's murder, Jamie handled the sale of the house. "I knew the people who lived in that house before the Willses," she told me later, "so when I offered it for sale, I could talk about other families who had lived and prospered there. It wasn't just 'the murder house.'" In addition, Jamie and her parents both lived in the neighborhood: her parents on Ambassador Drive and Jamie, with her husband and two young children, on Sandringham. At that time, Jamie was also president of the neighborhood association. Why I hadn't thought of approaching her sooner, I'm not sure.

When I called, she quickly agreed to let me interview her. I didn't get a chance to talk directly with her husband; a venture capitalist, he was often out of town scouting new business deals. But Jamie assured me he'd have no objection. I didn't mention sleeping over right away; those turndowns had made me even more cautious, and I figured I'd get to know Jamie better before popping that question.

Jamie's roots in the neighborhood were deep. Her parents moved to Houston Barnard when she was seventeen, so she had lived her last year of high school here. She even married here. "I love the neighborhood and I love the land here," she said later, explaining why she set her wedding at a friend's stately home in Houston Barnard. "My friend had an absolutely beautiful yard!" she said. She especially appreciated the visual elements that unified the neighborhood aesthetically: slate roofs; iron fences; traditional, harp-shaped streetlamps; and homes, driveways, and walkways of stone or brick. Her wedding ceremony was held precisely at 12:34 and 56 seconds p.m. on July 8, 1990, or—just as she'd planned—at "1234567890."

Set on the same side of Sandringham as me and about ten houses down, Jamie Columbus's own large and impressive home was in what is called the Cotswold Cottage style. Sometimes these homes are referred to as "storybook" houses because they look so much like traditional country houses often pictured in English children's books. Modern versions became popular in the United States in the 1920s and '30s; Jamie's house was built in 1926. Faced with stucco and half-timbering, the house had several gables, and a steep, slate roof meant to mimic the look of thatch. In the back was a large yard with a perennial English garden and an in-ground pool. Inside, Jamie's home was filled with colors, textures, and shapes. The dining room had a ruby-colored ceiling and a chandelier made of old copper plumbing fixtures, the breakfast room was blue, a small sitting room was green. Everywhere hung paintings, photographs in handmade frames, and what Jamie later described as "treasures from around the world": Asian lanterns, musical instruments, and a young Indian girl's dress. The TV cabinet was an ice box; there was an old church pew; furniture, including distressed farm pieces, was hand-painted.

Jamie, forty, was of medium build with dark blond hair that fell in soft curls to her shoulders. On that first visit, she wore vibrant colors and jewelry from Africa and India that made her almost appear to sparkle.

She showed me into the living room, where her daughter, Lily, three—with blondish-brown curls like her mother—sat at a child's table coloring on paper with pencils and marker. Her brother, Max, five, was at a Montessori school. Jamie's husband was at work.

"Lily and I are coproducing a book!" Jamie exclaimed. Jamie had a clear, soprano voice and often spoke in excited outbursts. "We're making portraits of the First Ladies. Each First Lady gets her own page and write-up. A whole book of them! Right now, we're on Coolidge."

Excusing herself to take a phone call, Jamie went to her study. Later, she told me the call was for a new business she and her mother were starting called "On the House," a real estate benefits program for corporations to offer their employees.

Jamie invited me to the kitchen, where she had already made us tea. She'd made cookies and prepared a fruit plate. If I slept over, I thought, breakfast was likely to be very good.

I commented on the art everywhere. Jamie acknowledged that most of the paintings—oil pastels—and color photographs were her own. She had traveled to more than thirty-six countries, she explained, in Central and South America, the Middle East, Europe, Africa, and Southeast Asia. Her purpose was to study, photograph, and paint "indigenous tribal women, how they live and the work they do." This was a different side of my neighbor than most people knew. To most town residents, Jamie Columbus was the Harvard Business School graduate who had come back to work at her mother's real estate firm—she'd had her own real estate license since she was eighteen. She was the face and name on countless FOR SALE signs in some of the more upscale neighborhoods in town—including ours.

But Jamie, I saw, was also an artist, someone who had graduated college with a double major in philosophy and psychology, had lived in New York City and kept her own painting studio, and who, in her free time, still loved to travel, photograph, and paint.

"I love the incredible beauty and color of women wearing traditional clothing," she continued, talking of her travels, "of seeing them harvesting, working in the fields, and in the markets."

Before they had children, Jamie and her husband took a trip around the world, visiting and helping support humanitarian projects. In one African village, Jamie saw "a mother, grandmother, and a man and all his wives living in huts right next to each other," she said. "In many cultures, your family is also your neighborhood.

"I'm lucky," she continued, "that Max and Lily's grandparents live so close. That's why I moved back to Rochester and to the neighborhood. We could get to their house just by running through several yards."

After our snack, Jamie offered to show me her studio on the third floor. I followed her up the stairs, which were made of walnut and had a runner made of sea grass and a border made of sewn pieces of Guatemalan tribal shirts.

In her studio were many paintings in progress; around the perimeter of the floor, photos leaned against the wall. Most of the photos, just as Jamie had described them, showed women and girls in their native environment. Almost always, women were pictured working: selling things in the market, carrying water, gathering food. They wore colorful robes, saris, or aprons, depending on location. Jamie had collected many of her photos into a book she called *Earth Tones Woman*. Just then, she explained, she was working to find a publisher.

One thing in particular intrigued me about Jamie's paintings: many of the women's faces were blank—they had no features at all. I asked about this.

"I have a strong feeling of the collective unconscious of women around the world," she said, "so in my paintings, it's more, 'Here are the women' versus 'Here is *a* woman with a particular face.' Look," she continued, "at Harvard Business School, women did not always work together, but in these other countries, women work together. It's women as a group that interests me, and what I found so beautiful about women working together is the community they form."

This prompted me to ask Jamie about the native villages themselves as communities. From her travels, I wondered, had she learned anything about how these villages are structured to form community?

"Can I borrow your notepad?" she asked, and then drew in pencil on a blank page.

"This is how a typical village is structured," she said, showing me the pad. She had drawn two concentric circles with little squares surrounding the inner one and lines radiating out from the center to each of the squares. Pointing to the little squares, she said, "These are the huts. They're all built around a point in the middle. It's like a lotus with petals radiating out."

Her drawing did, in fact, resemble the inside of a flower.

"Successful communities—'tribal neighborhoods,' if you want to think of it that way—ideally are built around a central space," she said. "It can be dirt, or mud, or green space. But it's central and it's where they gather."

Then Jamie drew a second sketch below the first. This one showed a heavy, horizontal line with two large boxes above it and two below. Inside each box was a smaller one. "This is how a typical American neighborhood is laid out," she said. The horizontal line was a street; the large boxes were lots, and the smaller boxes inside the lots were houses. "You see, people are contained within their own spaces—you don't even have to see the people closest around you—and there's no center.

"And there's another difference, too," she continued. "In other cultures, people live outside more. There's nothing to do in your house, so there's far fewer secrets. Here, ninety-nine percent of your day you're behind closed doors—especially in a climate like ours. And you're hidden behind three layers of protection: a front door, an alarm system, and you have thousands of square feet to spend time in.

"Traditionally, individual survival was not possible; you were dependent on others in your village for support. But in Western culture we think we can survive alone. Here you can go days or weeks, or literally years, without seeing the people in the house right next door.

"So the neighborhood"—and here I understood Jamie was speaking of our neighborhood—"may be unified by the consistency of building materials, but it certainly isn't unified in terms of the people who live here. This community is an archipelago; at times it feels as though everyone is on their own half-acre island."

Jamie's cell phone rang, and after taking the call—evidently from a real estate client—she ran down to her study to send another fax. It seemed a good time for me to leave, but we agreed to meet again soon.

AT the agreed-upon time at Starbucks, a week or two later, I waited for Jamie. It was a chilly afternoon, and I warmed myself with a cup of tea. As the minutes passed with no sign of her, I began to worry that she'd changed her mind about meeting with me. After twenty minutes, I called Jamie at home but there was no answer, and I didn't have her cell number. After half an hour, I began calculating how long I should stay before I could safely assume she wasn't going to show.

And then Jamie swooshed in, her silver earrings dangling under a Peruvian cap with ear flaps. She looked tired. After making apologies for being late—I'm not sure I really caught what had held her up—she got some tea and we resumed our earlier conversation.

I'd been thinking more about Jamie's description of the structure of native villages and how, in her view, it promotes community. But this was an American suburb and we weren't suddenly going to uproot our houses and reposition them around a central fire circle, so what, if anything, could actually be done, in her opinion, to improve a neighborhood like Houston Barnard?

"Our neighborhood needs certain things," she said, sipping her tea. "It needs a moms' group—some way for mothers with young children to get together. Where I lived growing up, we'd walk out of the house and there'd be moms and kids around. Here, if people go out, they go into their backyards. Not only aren't there front porches—they're against code—but you don't even see people if you look into their houses because the rooms on the front are usually the living and dining rooms, which usually are unused."

Speaking of "not seeing people," I wondered if she had ever seen Lou Guzzetta. Jamie asked if Lou was "that gray-haired man I've seen out walking."

So what would it take, I asked again, to redesign the neighborhood so people could actually see and know each other?

"Well, first I'd create a centralized park for families to gather." Though tired, Jamie's enthusiasm was building and we began speculating on which houses in the neighborhood with side lots—there were a handful—could sell their lots to the neighborhood association for a common park. "Of course, it would cost a half-million dollars for the lot," she noted, "and many neighbors haven't even joined the association, which is a twenty-dollar fee."

What else besides common space?

"I'd have some kind of official welcoming committee. And we need more neighborhood gatherings. In the park area there could be an artistic kind of bench or other seating for families and children to have a picnic or play a game.

"Look," she continued, "right now there's no forum for even discussing ideas about neighborhood beyond the instinctual one of protecting one's property and privacy. People's feeling is: they bought their houses; they didn't buy a percentage of the community."

Did Jamie feel that, as neighbors, we have an obligation to know each other to help prevent a tragedy like what happened to the Willses?

"Well, yes and no," she said. "There is an obligation to get involved if you see something wrong or spooky, but no, I don't believe there's any obligation to inquire."

Jamie then recalled how she'd learned of the shootings. "Someone called me and said there was a murder-suicide on Sandringham. Honestly, I didn't even know what a 'murder-suicide' was. Then when I found it was the Willses, I felt terrible. I wanted to do whatever I could to help, so I organized food delivery for the family."

She said soon after the shootings she had suggested a neighborhood meeting—she wasn't association president yet—but was told it would be inappropriate, so nothing happened.

"I had tried to get to know Renan when they first moved in," Jamie reflected, "but it wasn't easy. I couldn't find her Chi."

"Her Chi?"

"Her essence—in Buddhist philosophy, the center of her being," explained Jamie. "Renan was a tragedy. I wish we could have helped her."

Getting back to how to improve the neighborhood, Jamie had some more suggestions.

"We need to embrace people young and old, and from different ethnicities. We need some expression of a neighborhood—the American way would be to say 'team spirit' with neighborhood T-shirts or something. Houston Barnard T-shirts—right! And activities, like 'Houston Barnard goes to the YWCA to help women there.'

"It's so people don't live in a neighborhood that is made up just of homes, but is made of people in those homes that do things together. Here, for example, people spend Christmas at home with just family, but other places in the world people celebrate together, as a group. They make opportunities for celebration: new moon, holidays, even in the poorest of poor places, they find ways to come together. They have feasts."

I was curious how Jamie would respond to a point I'd made earlier when talking with Orhan Beckman, the psychologist and brother of Renan Wills: that public space in American has increasingly become privatized.

"You know," I said, "it seems more and more that where we can run into other people isn't a park or the village green, but a private, commercial space like the supermarket, or Barnes and Noble, or right here in Starbucks."

Jamie agreed. "Yes, but in those places you're not meeting people daily like you would in the village square, but randomly. If I see you at the supermarket, it's maybe once a month, and where am I going with that? What am I gonna say, 'Hi, how's

your fruit?' It's pleasant, but it's superficial. In traditional villages, especially when I slept over, I'd see people regularly, every
morning for example, washing their saris in the river."

"You *slept* in the villages?" I asked.

"Yeah, sometimes. Didn't I mention that? In some of these
villages, I stayed overnight."

"So you actually slept over, like in a hut?"

"Yeah, sometimes in a hut."

She named villages in Peru and Kenya, one near Lake Ati-
tlán in Guatemala, Chang Mai in Thailand, and one in the Atlas
Mountains in Morocco.

"And why'd you do that?"

"Because I find that with sleeping over, it's more meaningful," she said. "You get involved in people's lives more. You bond
with people and learn about their families."

If I had had any doubts that she'd say yes about the sleepover,
I now had none. If Jamie herself had experienced the bonding
of sleeping over, surely she'd agree that I could do the same at
her house.

"So what was it like?" I asked. "The sleeping over?"

"Well, to be honest, it can be uncomfortable," she said. "Usually, I'd sleep on a hard surface. There were the sounds of dogs in
the night—you really didn't want to go out to the bathroom, you
know? It could be a very long night, and then in the early morning there'd be roosters crowing. But the emotional and spiritual
experience transcended the hardship."

We were both mostly done with our tea. I didn't want to
ask Jamie just then about sleeping over—I'd save that for our
next meeting. But almost on a whim, I did ask her one more
question: in selling real estate in the area, had she found any
neighborhoods where people actually did have a "central green

space" or any kind of property in common? To my surprise, she not only said that she had, but offered to take me there.

And that was how, minutes later, I found myself driving behind Jamie's SUV, climbing a long, steep incline toward the local reservoir when suddenly Jamie took a sharp turn to the right into what looked like a driveway but was actually a side street. Moments later, I was parked behind her on a narrow road among a cluster of nearly a dozen houses. I'd lived in this general area much of my life, and never knew that little neighborhood was there.

"Isn't this cool? Isn't this great!" she gushed. The homes—Tudors, Colonials, and others built in the 1910s and '20s—sat on a hillside, bordering a public park. But the distinguishing feature, just as Jamie had said, was that this mini-neighborhood was indeed built around a central grassy area, which, she explained, all the neighbors owned. The common ownership was written into their property deeds—something Jamie knew about because she had recently been the listing agent for the sale of two of the houses.

"As far as I can tell," she said, "hardly anyone actually uses the common grassy area, but it could be wonderful."

JAMIE had gotten me wondering if I could find other examples of individual homeowners sharing property, and the ways in which they might gather together and make use of their common space. Later, a little research showed that, while it's not common, it does exist.

• "I'm lucky to live in Shore Acres," Dan Postotnik, a resident of that mixed-income Cleveland neighborhood on the shore of Lake Erie, wrote me. The 168 Shore Acres homeowners share two park properties, which are overseen and maintained by their neighborhood association. One of the parks, the size of a city lot, is used primarily as a playground. Neighborhood volunteers installed swings and slides, benches, and "a giant barbecue big enough for the whole neighborhood to celebrate together on the Fourth of July," according to association president Meg Doerr. The other property, covering three lots, had been used as a tennis court until recently when residents decided to convert it into another park with a large picnic shelter and community gardens. Residents pay just $50 annually to cover taxes and insurance on the two properties. Volunteers clean up the parks in spring and fall, removing tree branches and mulching around the playground.

The two shared parks are the center of neighborhood life, says Doerr. Some neighbors have held their weddings there, and recently many gathered in the park with one of Shore Acre's most senior residents to celebrate his ninety-first birthday. The association is considering buying an empty lot on the opposite end of the neighborhood to create yet a third park, and also buying a vacant home to rent out to artists for living and studio space—a way to encourage arts in the neighborhood. "It takes effort and commitment to nurture and maintain such a community," notes Postotnik, "but we prove it can be done, despite the broad changes in the society around us."

• In the historic Center Square–Hudson Park neighborhood of Albany, New York, owners of six adjoining brick row houses have traded a bit of privacy for a lot of beautiful gardening. "Our tiny backyards were really shaded from the stockade fences between each unit," recalls one of the owners, Kathryn Sikule. "With the shade from the fences, you really couldn't grow too much." Beginning in 2006, Sikule and some of her neighbors came up with the idea of taking down the fences and combining their gardens.

Over time, more neighbors agreed to take down their fences or trellises and merge gardens. The result was "a beautiful, unique garden that has brought us all together as a community," says Sikule. Stone foot paths set among the joint garden allow each resident access to the full landscaped space, and an uninterrupted view of a sunny, garden scene filled with plants, shrubs, and annual flowers. Already, some of the original neighbors have moved away but the new owners have accepted the joint garden, says Sikule. In an article about the garden, writer Jane Gottlieb observed, "For about the same amount of work, each [owner] gets five times the yard and a kinship that gates and posts would never have allowed."

• In Southern California, residents of Avondale, a mixed-income retirement community in the town of Palm Desert, worked together to create a dog park. According to eleven-year resident Cheryle Clark, the park quickly "has become a gathering spot not only for the dogs, but their owners, too." One resident, William Gazecki, eyeing an unused, triangular-shaped lot near the gated community's golf course—unsuitable for a home because of traffic on one side and a wall on the other—donated enough money for fencing and labor. Another resident covered the costs for plantings, and others held a raffle to raise funds for maintenance. Now, says Cheryle Clark, twenty to forty dogs use the park regularly, often half a dozen at a time. "Absolutely," she says, "it creates a community feel. And if someone is new and they have a dog, they can bring it to the park and other people immediately meet them."

Clark explained another benefit: "We have a lot of older people here, and now with the park—at least with the dog owners—we pretty much see each other daily. One morning, some of the dog owners felt one of the older people didn't look so well. They checked him out and then called 911. That happened directly because they gathered together at the dog park."

• Summers are not overly long in western New York State, but in East Irondequoit, a Rochester suburb, seven families who collectively own an in-ground pool enjoy the season by swimming and socializing with neighbors. As the neighborhood developed in the 1960s, explains current resident Phil Townsend, homeowners purchased an available property, set up a not-for-profit corporation, and built the pool. The result has been, says Townsend, "a neighborhood jewel."

Among the seven families, Townsend estimates about twenty-five adults and children use the pool. "It's been the key to the neighborhood being the type of place where everyone knows and watches out for each other," he says. "And you don't just know who the neighbors are; you know each other very well because you sit at the pool and chat: 'Gee, how's your mom doing in the hospital? How's your daughter doing at college?' That sort of thing."

To keep up the pool, each family pays about $500 to $600 annually to cover taxes, chemicals, and other maintenance. Families share maintenance chores. Only rarely, says Townsend, does anyone fail to do their jobs or to follow the pool rules. "It's like having your own pool, and the great thing is you can use it anytime but if you want to go out of town you don't have to worry about it."

* * *

JAMIE and I met a third time a week later on a Monday after-noon at her home. Max and Lily were at school. As before, she had prepared tea and cookies.

Jamie asked if I would like to go up to her studio; she had some new paintings to show me. I decided that while we were upstairs, that would be the time to ask about sleeping over.

In her studio, Jamie showed me a canvas of two zebras stand-ing on an African plain. The animals' necks were intertwined in a romantic way that made their stripes mesh. There was a time not so long ago—right after Marie and I had separated—when it would have pained me just to see that painting—but now I could enjoy it.

What had changed was that I'd recently started seeing some-one: a lovely woman named Marla. Our families had known each other—her daughter and my daughters were close in age—and she, too, had recently divorced. Marla was bright, attractive, and had a good job in education. I made a mental note to ask Jamie later if I could buy the zebra painting—I knew she occasionally offered her work for sale, and it would make a nice gift for Marla.

Many other canvasses leaned against the walls. I wanted to ask Jamie again about the women without faces—she'd said ear-lier the reason was to depict women in general rather than any woman in particular. But I was still curious about a busy, ac-complished woman like Jamie going halfway around the world to paint women working and then make their faces blank—just smudges, really.

"I think it also has to do with just trying to represent the sim-plicity of native life," she began, in answer to my renewed question. "I go to these places to try to learn from these women, to learn about the simplicity of their lives. I live a complicated life, I know, but I seek a simple one. I paint people who I strive to be like."

Jamie did lead a complicated life. Her face and name were on hundreds of FOR SALE signs all over town, and each time I'd come to her home, I'd watch her juggle business calls, e-mails, and faxes, and a slew of other projects: soliciting publishers for her photography book, now running the neighborhood association, starting yet another real estate company with her mother, organizing—as she'd recently told me—her fifteenth reunion for Harvard Business School, plus constantly creating home educational projects—like the book of First Ladies—for Max and Lily. And just that day she'd said she was beginning to plan a trip to Bhutan.

"So, have you had much luck simplifying things?" I asked.

"Well, right now," she said, "if you really want to know, I'm sort of going through a crisis."

That sounded like the prelude to Deb O'Dell's "meltdown" story in the car. I hoped Jamie wasn't going in the same direction.

"I'm trying to get rid of unessential things, of the noise in my life," she explained. "Trying to see what I want to do next."

I asked if her husband was supportive of her efforts.

"Not really," she said, and then paused.

"To be honest," she continued. "I've been trying to figure out if I want to stay married."

"I'm sorry," I said.

Then Jamie revealed that the reason she'd been late to our meeting the previous week at Starbucks was because she had decided that day to proceed with a divorce. I remembered how tired she'd looked when she came in.

I asked how she was doing.

She was sleep-deprived, she said, and overwhelmed taking care of the kids. She was trying to exercise a lot.

"I hope you won't mind me asking," I said, "but are there any weapons in the house?"

In fact, I found it difficult to imagine either Jamie or her husband owning a gun, but the Willses' shootings were still very much on my mind, and so my question to Jamie was serious.

"I'm amused by the question, almost," she said, smiling. "Our home is a weapons-free zone!"

I told Jamie she could call me at any hour of the day or night, or just come over if for any reason she didn't feel safe.

We talked more that afternoon about painting and photography and about neighborhoods in general, but I knew I wouldn't be sleeping over. Her family was in crisis, and this was no time for an overnight guest.

Before I left that day, Jamie excused herself—she needed to get something from the basement. I waited in the kitchen, but then a moment later heard her shriek a string of profanities.

"What is it? What's the matter?" I shouted in response.

"There's water all over this floor!" she yelled, and then cursed again.

I went down to take a look. There were puddles on the basement floor, but they weren't "all over," they were just in spots. There must have been a leak after a heavy rain the previous night. Jamie, I supposed, was understandably a bit fragile from the weighty decision she'd made, from lack of sleep, and from anxiety over the steep road ahead.

6

The Woman in the Castle

PATTI DiNitto's connecting flight from Chicago arrived in Rochester at 9:20 p.m., nearly an hour late due to bad weather in the West. She'd called earlier to let me know she'd be delayed, and also to say that her older daughter, Caitlin, eleven, would be sleeping at home that night.

Patti was one of the last passengers off the plane. As she walked from the arrival gate down the long corridor toward the terminal, I spotted her easily: a petite woman—5 foot 3 and slender—in jeans and black leather jacket. She moved slowly but steadily, holding a purse and pulling a small suitcase behind her.

We hugged in a friendly way. I offered to carry her bag, but she declined.

Beneath the leather jacket, she wore several layers. "I'm cold unless it's eighty degrees," she said. It wasn't eighty degrees. It was February in Rochester—a summer and fall had gone by since my last sleepover—and it hadn't been much above twenty degrees all week. After three days in California, the contrast must have been difficult for her. In my car, I turned the heat up all the way and ran the blower on high, then asked where she'd like to go for dinner. "I don't want to make any decisions," she said. She explained she was tired, although not from the medical procedures, just from traveling.

"Your car smells like dog," she said with a smile. "I'm going to get you an air freshener."

There was nothing wrong with Patti's sense of smell, nor her sense of humor. In fact, the car did smell like dog; I'd had Champ in there the other day when I took him to a park.

I drove to a strip mall five minutes from Sandringham Road. Patti waited in the car with the engine running while I went to see which restaurants were open. It was five minutes to ten; everything was closed except Applebee's.

The restaurant ("America's Favorite Neighbor," as it calls itself) had opened just a few weeks earlier; this was my first visit. A young hostess in a T-shirt that read APPLEBEE'S: YOUR NEIGHBORHOOD HEADQUARTERS showed us to a booth. A waitress wearing a HI, NEIGHBOR! button brought us menus and ice water. Then, over the din of a sports show from a wall-mounted TV, Patti told me about her trip to the San Francisco Medical Center, where she was a participant in the trial of an experimental breast cancer vaccine.

Two years ago, as a radiologist specializing in mammography, Patti, then thirty-nine, had diagnosed her own breast cancer. "I had had a mammogram at thirty-five," she told me. "The recommendation at the time was for the next one at forty, but it was obvious something was wrong. I did a mammogram, then had a biopsy."

The timing was especially difficult: ten months before, Patti's husband had moved out, leaving her with two girls in a four-bedroom, 4,500-square-foot home on Sandringham Road.

Patti had a soft, high-pitched voice; over the TV, it was especially difficult to hear her.

How Patti managed to get herself into the cancer vaccine trial in San Francisco was all about determination. Researching on the Internet, she told me, she discovered Dendreon, a biotechnology firm based in Seattle developing targeted therapies for cancer. The company was about to begin testing a vaccine aimed at Patti's type of breast cancer, known as HER-2/neu. Chemotherapy and radiation had put her cancer in remission; the vaccine, if it worked, might keep it that way.

But the company discouraged Patti from traveling to California, where the drug trial was being conducted. Participants, the doctors pointed out, would have to come to San Francisco monthly for a year, first for treatments and then for follow-ups, and the costs of travel and lodging would not be reimbursed. Yet Patti flew out anyway to meet with the principal researcher. She insisted she'd be a good candidate and promised if she were allowed into the study—there was just one opening left—that she would pay her own way.

Once a month for the past six months, Patti had flown to San Francisco for treatments. The first round of measurements didn't show any positive results, but Patti said it was still too early to know. She hoped to have some good news after her trip the next month.

While in San Francisco, Patti stayed with the sister of a Rochester businessman named Scott whom Patti had been dating for about a year. For Patti, her new friendship with Scott's sister, and the ability to have a home away from home while receiving treatments, had been two good aspects of what otherwise was a tiring monthly ordeal. The first I heard that this arrangement was in jeopardy had come in a phone call from Patti about two weeks earlier, at around 10:30 at night.

"I'm kinda bummed," she said in her birdlike voice.

I was concerned. In the weeks since my first meeting with her, as I was doing some background interviews, Patti seldom called me, and never so late in the evening.

"Are you feeling okay?" I asked.

"Yeah."

"News from California okay?" I thought maybe she had received some bad news about the vaccine trial.

"Yeah, as much as they can tell," she said. "It's sort of early to know how it's doing."

"So what's got you so bummed?"

"My boyfriend," she said, pausing. "It kinda didn't work out, I guess."

"Oh, I'm sorry," I said. "When did this happen?"

"It's been a tough week," she said. "Men are such . . ." And then her voice trailed off.

Not only was Patti crushed by the breakup with Scott, but she was afraid she'd no longer be able to stay in San Francisco with his sister, and she had six more trips coming up. As it turned out, however, Scott's sister was glad to continue the friendship. So that night at Applebee's, Patti told me she stayed with Scott's sister the previous two nights. "We had a lot of fun," she said. "It's like a pajama party."

"Good friends are hard to come by," she added.

I asked if while she was away she had heard from Scott. There was a pause, and then she said, "No," and she didn't say anything more.

I was overcome with all Patti had suffered in the last couple of years: divorce, cancer, the leave of absence from her job, then the boyfriend.

"You've had to deal with a lot of losses," I said.

"Yeah," she said with a sigh. "But, hey, they didn't happen all at once."

"Where do you get the strength?"

"I think it's just how you're put together," she said. "I am disappointed in how my life has turned out. But then, I suppose I could have had this fine, healthy life and good marriage, and got hit by a car. I mean, we don't know how things are going to end up, so who's to say this life is worse than some alternative?"

When we left Applebee's, I saw that as she walked, Patti dragged her left leg a little. I'd seen her do this a few other times when she had been tired or we had walked a lot. She said it was from the chemo; for a while after the last round of treatments, she had used a cane. The parking lot was dark and there were patches of ice, so to steady her on the way to my car, I took her arm.

I don't recall when I first heard about Patti; it seemed that over several months, a few neighbors mentioned to me a doctor who lived down the street who was ill. One heard she'd diagnosed her own disease and then given up her practice; another thought she was divorced with a couple of kids. I couldn't locate anyone, however, who actually knew her.

At the O'Dells' one day, I asked Dave and Deb if they recognized the name of one of our neighbors, Dr. Patricia DiNitto. They didn't.

Dave asked where she lived.

"Well," I said. "That's an interesting thing. I looked her up in the directory and she lives really close: just two doors down from you—three from me—on our same side of the street."

"Oh, the castle!" said Dave.

All three of us knew the house well—it was one of the handsomest on the street. Constructed of sand-colored stones, it had a slate roof and, built around the front door, a two-story turret.

Dave said he'd never met the people who lived there, but he sometimes had seen a child outside in the morning waiting for the school bus.

I wanted to meet Dr. DiNitto. I was curious about her and upset to think a single mother with breast cancer might be living three doors down from me and I knew nothing about her.

But how to reach her? Her home number, I soon learned, was unlisted and I didn't think it would be proper—or effective— just to show up at her door.

I called Lou Guzzetta. He was a doctor; maybe he knew her. "Never have heard of her," he said. "Should I?"

Jamie Columbus also said she hadn't met her.

Through an Internet search, I found Dr. DiNitto's radiology office. It was one of the premier mammography centers in town. Her entry on the website included a curriculum vitae and a photograph. The vitae, which ran four pages, listed many honors and awards, publications, and other distinctions. The photograph showed a young, smiling woman, head tilted self-assuredly to one side. When I called the office, a receptionist told me Dr. DiNitto was on a leave of absence.

I needed her home phone number but I also needed an introduction, perhaps from a mutual friend. I asked friends who were doctors but couldn't find anyone who knew Dr. DiNitto well enough to introduce me.

As a last resort, I sent an e-mail to the address listed in the neighborhood directory: "I live a couple of houses down from you on Sandringham. I'm a writer and am interested in talking with you in regard to a project I'm working on. Could I give you a call sometime?" Three days later, I received a reply: "Sure, I would like to help if I can," and she included her home phone number. The next day, I called. We chatted briefly and set up a date to meet at her home the next Sunday afternoon.

When Sunday came, I was just putting on my coat to walk over to Patti DiNitto's house when she called to say that wouldn't work. Instead, she would come to my house.

The Patti DiNitto at my front door looked strikingly different from the healthy, vigorous person pictured in her photograph on the clinic website: her once full face was now thin, and her hair was sparse.

"I went through the hair loss twice," she told me later. "My hair was straight and somewhat wavy, but now it's just curls."

Patti agreed right away with my concerns about the neighborhood: she'd lived on the street five years, she said, and hadn't met a single person, and found it both curious and frustrating. Consequently, she said she had been glad to get my e-mail and would be happy to cooperate with my request to spend time together and write about her. Over the next few weeks, we met several times to talk—went shopping together and had a few other outings—and later when I proposed a sleepover, she agreed without hesitation. She also told me why at the last minute she'd changed the location of our first meeting: after her husband left, she said, she had never finished decorating the house—the dining room, for example, was bare—and she was embarrassed about that.

*   *   *

PATTI'S home—"the castle," as Dave O'Dell called it—was built in 1930, in the French Eclectic style then popular in American residential architecture. From the central turret's second floor, a bay of casement windows faced the street. The style borrows both from French country estates and earlier Gothic design.

Following our late dinner, I drove back to Patti's, parked, and carried Patti's suitcase and my overnight bag into the house. We said good night to the babysitter, who'd been staying with Patti's daughter Caitlin. It was nearly midnight; Caitlin was already asleep in her room upstairs.

Then Patti took me up the back stairway, just off the back hall, to show me where I'd be sleeping. The room was once a maid's room but recently Patti's brother, Joe, a carpenter and cabinetmaker, had remodeled it. "I couldn't do any of this without Joey," she said. Her brother, she explained, was between jobs when Patti's husband left, and Joe did all the work to fix up the house: he raised the ceilings, built the cabinetry, and remodeled the kitchen. The maid's room, with Joe's renovations, now had built-in closets, cabinets, and bookshelves; a private, connecting bath; casement windows facing front and back; and a double bed. Most important for me on that cold winter night, the room—which sat above the garage—was now well insulated and warm.

While Patti checked on Caitlin, I went back down to the kitchen. The counter and tabletops, I noticed, were clean and free of clutter—something I was rarely able to achieve in my own house. Just then, Patti surprised me by entering the kitchen from the other direction—she must have come down the main stairway.

"So what do we do next? Want to watch TV or read?" she asked.

We were two single adults in her house late at night, alone except for her daughter asleep upstairs. The situation, and indeed, the whole relationship, was ripe for confusion.

The potential for misunderstanding had first surfaced a few weeks earlier. One night, as she was arriving home from a previous trip to San Francisco, I'd picked her up at the airport. It was almost midnight, but she was full of energy and wanted to go out for a drink to celebrate having completed four monthly vaccine infusions. I rarely go to bars and had no idea where to take her, but she had a friend who owned a bar in a nearby suburb, so we went there. In a back room, near a fireplace, we found a quiet table. I got a martini for her and a beer for me, and we began to talk. I encouraged her to tell me about her childhood.

She said her parents had both immigrated from a village in Italy—her father at nine years old and her mother, later, at nineteen—and that their marriage in Rochester had been arranged. Her family lived in Greece, New York, a mostly blue-collar Rochester suburb, and she was the fourth of five children. Her father was an engineer and instrument maker at Eastman Kodak—he worked on the original lunar module, Patti said; her mother was a homemaker. In school, math and science had come easily to Patti and she thought of a career in medicine, but her father dissuaded her—he thought it would take too much time and be too risky. He wanted her to be an accountant. Dutifully, Patti began college as a business major, but then switched to pre-med, later becoming the first person in her family to graduate college and also to attend medical school. Through all her schooling, she paid her own way, ending up with one of the highest debt loads of anyone in her medical school class.

At medical school, Patti did well, but she found the environment difficult. "A couple of the profs just didn't like me," she recalled. "I was shy and didn't speak up. What they liked to see was people's claws out, being aggressive and trying to outdo one another, but that's not my personality."

While we spoke at the bar, I asked Patti if her father had lived to see her become a doctor. She paused, and her eyes began to tear.

"No," she said. "He died after my first year of college. He was just fifty-nine." She paused again. "Maybe that's why I do everything I can so each of the kids can spend time with their father, because I felt like I didn't get to—like I was shortchanged."

I was struck by the many similarities between Patti's life and that of Deb O'Dell. Both had come from modest backgrounds and then excelled academically; ambitious and hardworking, both had been inspired by their fathers' dreams for them, yet both had lost their fathers early, before they themselves had achieved their professional goals. And despite so much in common, Patti and Deb, who had lived two doors down from each other for three years, had never met.

"I'm sorry," she said. "I cry easily. After chemo, like after having a baby, it's easy to cry at sentimental things."

It was at that moment I saw just how confusing our relationship could become. I needed to establish for both of us that I was a friend, not a suitor. So I made a point that night in the bar to tell Patti about Marla, the woman I'd recently begun dating. I told her how often I saw Marla, how happy it made me to be with her, and how our relationship seemed to be deepening. Patti said she was glad for me.

*   *   *

NOW, weeks later, there we were: self-consciously standing around in the kitchen, trying to figure out what to do next. To her question about whether I wanted to read or watch TV, I replied, "What would you normally do if I wasn't here?"

"Well, if you weren't here," she said, "I'd go upstairs, unpack my clothes, and go to bed."

"Then you should do that," I said. "Just do what you would normally do."

"But I want to be a good host," she said.

"I'll read in the living room while you unpack," I said. "How'll that be?"

Patti said it would be fine.

THE living room featured leaded, casement windows, dark wood paneling, and French doors that, in the summer months, opened onto a backyard patio. A fire burned in a marble-fronted gas fireplace. In the middle of the room were playthings for her younger daughter, five-year-old Sarah, including a children's play table with pink wooden chairs with backs shaped like crowns. Sarah was sleeping at her father's that night.

As I sank into a leather sofa to read the paper, I suddenly took in the situation as an outsider might see it: a tranquil, domestic scene with Patti in her room upstairs unpacking, Caitlin asleep in her room, and me relaxing in the living room with the newspaper. It felt complete in a way that life in my own house used to feel but didn't anymore. I wondered if it felt complete in that way for Patti, too.

Patti came downstairs. She was done unpacking. "Well, I guess it's time for us to go to bed," I said in a voice that even to me sounded husbandly. She turned off the living room lights, but left the pilot in the gas fireplace burning; it gave the room a dim glow. At the top of the stairs, we said good night. Patti said she'd be up around 6:30, in time to get Caitlin ready for school. She went to her room, which was on one end of the house, and I went to the maid's room, which was on the other end, and Caitlin was asleep in the middle.

THE front window of my room faced directly onto Sandringham where the street intersects with Ambassador Drive. That's the spot, Patti told me earlier, where she had seen a news truck parked on the night Bob Wills killed Renan and himself. Patti recalled it this way: "A patient of mine had been calling and calling that night and I just decided not to answer the phone anymore. I knew it could wait until the morning, so I didn't pick up. Later—I forget what time—I finally did answer because the phone wouldn't stop ringing. It turned out it was my brother, Joey. He had seen the eleven o'clock news and one of the TV stations had showed a picture of *our house* and he was thinking the murder was here. It wasn't impossible to believe because my husband and I at that time were going through a rough period."

Patti and her husband had moved to Sandringham only a few months before. She told me, "I was thinking to myself, 'Gee, we just bought a house in this neighborhood and now a murder?' In a way, though, that really started the divorce process for us. We separated about two months later."

Five years earlier, Patti had married on a summer weekend on the shore of Lake Ontario. She kept her family name, DiNitto, she said, because her husband wouldn't let her take his. When I asked her if that wasn't a little unusual, she said, "Looking

back, yes. I don't think he was ever planning to stay married."
They lived first in a small, two-bedroom condo in Greece, the suburb where Patti grew up, and then after Sarah was born, they moved to Brighton. With her radiologist's salary, Patti bought the house on her own, in her own name. "I went from never having a house to having a house on Sandringham," she said.

They had just begun decorating their new home when the marriage ran into trouble. "I wouldn't ever know he was mad or upset about something, and then he'd just kind of explode and leave the house," she recalled. "Once, I took his car keys because I wanted him to sit down and tell me what was wrong, but he called the police and said I was beating him up. He's a big guy and I was in my stocking feet. The police came and realized he's so big there's no way I was beating him up. They came at least twice; it was embarrassing. I thought to myself, 'Oh my God, the neighbors are going to think I'm a nutcase.'"

Her husband left on a Sunday afternoon. "I was at work the next morning seeing patients about their breast lumps," Patti recalled, "and all I wanted to do was scream, 'Hey, my husband left yesterday, and I've got no one to watch my kids. My life is falling apart here!'"

Suddenly, Patti had a lot to take care of on her own, including a large, still unfurnished home. "I really can't thank my brother enough," she told me. "He was at my house twenty-four/seven. He helped with everything." Patti also didn't know how things "were done" on Sandringham. "I didn't even realize people had lawn services. I mean, where I grew up, people cut their own grass. I asked Joey, 'Are the neighbors going to throw us out? I don't want to do anything incorrect here.' I was almost afraid to walk into my own front yard. Would people be checking us out?"

I asked Patti what she thought might have caused Bob Wills to do what he had done. "I'm sure being a surgeon is very stressful, and then when you have your wife leaving you . . ." she began, not finishing the thought. "If his friends weren't helping him . . ." she tried again. "Was he finally pushed to the limit?" she asked. "If it wasn't for my brother helping me, who knows?" She continued, "I felt an empathy. I felt it could have happened to me—I mean, going over the edge in some way. I was praying in thanks that it didn't."

Patti's brother had done a fine job remodeling the guest room. There was even a light over the bed that made it easy to read. Before I turned it off, I called Marla. Lately, whether I was sleeping at home or at a neighbor's, hers was my last call of the night. I recounted everything that had happened that evening since I picked Patti up at the airport, heard about her day at work and with her teenage daughter, and wished her a sweet good night.

MY cell phone alarm went off at 6 a.m. I showered and dressed and then sat on the bed waiting for Patti and Caitlin to get up. Patti had told me she gets up first, then wakes Caitlin and quickly makes Caitlin's bed "because otherwise she'll get back in it."

With each of the sleepovers, that was often my favorite moment: the first instant in the morning when I greeted my neighbors and wished them "good morning" inside their own houses, often upstairs in a hallway. The intimacy created by that one act would often set the tone for the whole day.

At 6:20 I heard an odd sound, like waves hitting a beach. I opened the door to my room and, down the hall, saw Patti, dressed in silk pajamas—emerge from Caitlin's room. "Caitlin's alarm," she said, "is supposed to sound like ocean waves. Unfortunately, it wakes me before it wakes her."

I followed Patti down the back stairway to the kitchen. She brought in the *Rochester Democrat and Chronicle*, turned on a light, and suggested I wait there while she and Caitlin got dressed.

On the counter were a newsletter, "Contemporary Diagnostic Radiology," a Lotto ticket, and a photo of Caitlin on an amusement park roller coaster ride with a man Patti later told me was her former boyfriend, Caitlin's father. She told me she remained on good terms with the fathers of both her daughters.

In fact, the only mild criticism I'd ever heard her express about Caitlin's dad was that he didn't take Caitlin to church often enough. Patti was concerned Caitlin might not meet her requirements for confirmation in the Catholic Church. Patti herself attended church most Sundays.

"I don't think I'd stand on a street corner and pass out Bibles," she told me when I asked her once about her faith. "Religion is just a personal thing for me, to help me in life. And that's what I want for my kids—just to have a faith. We happen to be Catholic—if you don't want to practice it, that's fine. If you'd rather study the Jewish faith, that's fine. It's just something to fall back on."

My favorite item in the kitchen was a wall calendar made of wood to resemble a little house. On the top was painted "Patti's Place," and then there were tiny, hand-painted wooden tiles that one could place over special days: a pumpkin for Halloween, an apple and book for the first day of school, a tie for Father's Day. It was February, and the tile over Valentine's Day—just a few days away—was a single red rose.

Off the kitchen was the dining room, which remained empty except for an area rug and, against one wall, an end table and a wooden chair.

I heard Patti's quiet voice at the top of the back stairway. "How come you're not going downstairs?" she asked her daughter, laughing. Caitlin must have been shy about meeting me. "Okay," said Patti. "I'll go down first!"

Caitlin was on crutches, having recently hurt her leg skiing. Whether she had a sprain or a chipped bone, Patti wasn't sure; they'd get an X-ray later in the week. Either way, Patti was confident her daughter would heal well. But she was concerned about plans to go to Arizona with both her daughters the following week for a school break. They were planning an active vacation: swimming, horseback riding, tennis, and riding dune buggies in the desert. Much of that would be difficult with Caitlin on crutches.

Caitlin sat at the kitchen table, dressed for school and waiting quietly while her mother heated frozen French toast.

I was surprised at how quiet and calm it all seemed, because Patti once described their morning get-off-to-school routine as "chaotic." One recent morning, she told me, she had even found herself thinking, "Oh, my God. I'm so glad Peter isn't here to see this!" But that morning, all was tranquil. Maybe it was because one daughter rather than two were home. Or more likely, it was because I was there and they were both on good behavior. I tried to lighten the mood.

"I feel like I should be serving you both breakfast, since I slept in the maid's room," I said. The joke, deservedly, fell flat.

I tried another conversation opener, mentioning to Caitlin, a sixth grader at the Brighton Middle School, that forty years ago I had attended the same school. This seemed to break the ice, and while she ate, Caitlin and I talked about life in middle school.

With her crutches, Caitlin couldn't climb the steps onto the school bus, so after breakfast we all hustled into Patti's SUV to drive to school—a five-minute ride. At the school parking lot, I carried Caitlin's backpack and violin case, while Patti helped with the crutches.

AT a restaurant near the middle school, Patti and I each ordered bagels for breakfast. On the tables were tiny, painted ceramic flowerpots. "Oh, look," I joked as we sat down. "They're giving away flowerpots for Valentine's Day."

"That's probably the only thing I'll get for Valentine's Day," said Patti.

I'd momentarily forgotten she was still hurting from the breakup with her boyfriend. Two weeks ago, I made a similar gaffe when I asked what plans she had for her birthday. "Big birthday," she replied. "Would you want to celebrate a birthday after your boyfriend dumps you?"

People all around us seemed to be having business conversations over breakfast.

"Mostly men here," I observed.

"Actually, that's why I come here!" she said, and then added, "Just kidding."

Patti seemed tired, and I had to strain to hear her.

I said how nice it was that she had the time to take Caitlin to school in the morning and help her get to class. She said it wasn't always so. "I didn't have any time when I was working," she said. "I'd be dropping two kids off at day care or schools, racing to the clinic, then having a hellacious schedule of patients."

My comment seemed to have touched a nerve.

"One morning I had Caitlin in the car to drop off at school," Patti continued, "and I whizzed right by the school forgetting to stop, and she said, 'Mom, aren't you going to drop me off?' So I raced back and dropped her off and then at work I got a call—there wasn't any school that day! I'm sure it was on the calendar, but it was the middle of the week. I was living a crazy life. I never want to do that again. Anybody who does that needs to see a psychologist."

The clinic where Patti worked employed six other full- and part-time radiologists, all women. Patti typically worked nine or ten hours a day, saw about thirty of her own patients and helped review mammograms of fifty others. When her cancer was diagnosed, she went on leave, but later thought of returning. "I was just coming out of my chemo and I felt okay and wanted my job back," she told me earlier. "I thought I could really help these women. Patients are totally confused, and most times doctors don't have firsthand experience with an illness, but I did. I thought I could give them a sense of hope, understanding, and encouragement, show them how to go from one step to the next, even just to say, 'You don't have to commit yourself to a course of treatment right away, you can think things through.'"

Patti's doctors thought full-time work might be too strenuous, but felt she could handle part-time. Patti called her boss. "She goes, 'Why don't you come in and we'll have a meeting with the lawyers.'" But the meeting never took place. "She called me back and said it wouldn't work. If I did anything wrong, patients would come down hard on me because they knew I'd been treated for cancer. They'd take advantage of me. She said I wouldn't be able to walk the halls there without somebody accusing me of malpractice."

Patti decided not to pursue it. "What I'd end up with wouldn't be worth the emotional and financial drain," she concluded, but the look in her eyes showed how bewildered and angry her boss's decision had left her.

"Well, she wasn't that swell when I worked there," she added, reflecting on her boss.

The previous week Patti had received an offer to join a radiology practice part-time. I asked if she was considering it.

"No," she said. "I'm burned out. I always thought medicine was to help people"—and here her quiet voice dropped even further to a conspiratorial whisper—"but it's not. It's all political. You don't get to be your own boss. You don't have time to observe the patients. You have to do what other people say, and even they're not the ones in charge—it's some businessman trying to get you to read films quickly. They just want you to read films until you fall out of the chair."

Fortunately, Patti's disability insurance now gave her enough money not to work and still afford to keep her home. In all our time together, she never expressed concern about finances.

But professionally, she wasn't sure what she wanted to do. At times, she expressed a sense of being confined by career choices made long ago.

"I don't ever want to work for someone else again," she declared, but then noted how difficult it was, given the cost of equipment and training staff, to open one's own radiology practice. "I could switch careers," she added. "Maybe I'll meet someone else in the book you're writing who can give me an idea—anyone in the neighborhood switch careers?"

No one came to mind, I said.

Then Patti turned more somber.

"All my life I've done what I should—getting good grades,

doing well in med school, working hard. I never rebelled as a teenager. I want to do something wild. I want to be bad."

But what "wild" or "bad" would look like, she was unable to say. Once, she mentioned a friend who'd ridden a motorcycle across country. Another time, at a local botanical garden, as we sat on a bench amid exotic flowers in a tropical setting, Patti said to me, "I still want to do something bad."

"Like what?" I asked.

"Like take off my clothes and run under the waterfall?" she teased.

"You go first," I said.

Back at the restaurant, eyeing the flowerpot on the table, I asked Patti in a more serious tone if Valentine's Day would, in fact, be difficult for her. She went cross-eyed. I laughed out loud—it was a funny look, and not what I would have expected from her. She blushed in embarrassment, but I think she enjoyed making me laugh.

I asked, "How did our fellow residents of Sandringham respond to your being ill?"

"Our street?" she asked, her eyes going wide. "No one talks to each other. I don't know anybody."

Patti said she knew one family on an adjacent street whose daughter went to kindergarten with Sarah, but as far as residents of Sandringham, she still didn't know anyone and hadn't heard from anyone.

"Do you suppose people on Sandringham know about your illness?" I asked.

"Oh, I suppose so," she said. "I think the word is probably around."

As I'd learned, it was.

"So how does it feel," I asked, "to be surrounded by people who know your difficult situation but who are not available to talk to, or to be of any help or comfort?"

Had I put it too harshly?

"When I got sick," she said, "I knew there were people around, but . . ." then she stopped.

"At the beginning," she started again, "it was okay with me. I didn't want anyone to see what my life was—what a catastrophe it was—an ongoing catastrophe."

Her eyes welled up.

"Because all the neighbors were strangers?" I offered.

She cried more and wiped her eyes with the napkin.

"I'm sorry," she said. "I'm just hypersensitive after the chemo. I think it's from all the tears I held back in college and med school and residency."

She continued, "At some point, I just didn't want them to help me."

I thought Patti was going to say she didn't want the neighbors' help because she resented us being so unneighborly, but actually she was going down a different path.

"Even with my friends who did help," she said, "I appreciated what they did, but I didn't like people in my house watching me lie around on the couch. I wanted them to see me healthy. I don't want people to feel sorry for me."

I asked how her friends had reacted to her illness.

"You get all kinds," she said. "Some feel sorry for you, some want to do a lot for you, and some are just nosy."

Was I one of the nosy ones? I didn't ask.

"And some people irritate me," she continued. "'Oh, poor Patti,'" she said, mock-patting her own arm. "I don't want to be 'poor-Pattied.' I really don't like people helping me out. I'd rather fix it myself."

But where did that leave the rest of us? What *should* neighbors do?

"Patti," I asked. "Let's say you live on a street where some people are casual acquaintances and others are just strangers. Yet all or most of them have heard about your divorce and illness. If they want to be good neighbors, what should they do?"

She thought for a long moment, then said, "I think just to call or e-mail some expression of caring. That would be enough."

AFTER breakfast, Patti and I drove back to Sandringham. As she pulled into her driveway, I gestured toward a large house on an adjacent street. The people who lived there were known to entertain a lot, especially outdoors in the summer.

"Some parties they have, huh?" I said.

"Oh, yeah. The best was their big anniversary," she said.

I remembered that party. Cars were lined up and down the street. Patti recalled all the details.

"People came in limos," she said. "They had valet parking. Everyone was in tuxedos and long gowns. Tables were set in the back with white tablecloths. A band played quiet dinner music but then at ten o'clock"—and here she made a dancing motion in the car seat—"it was like 'Devil in a Blue Dress'— really rockin'! The windows in my house were rattling, and I'm thinking 'Hey, it would be nice to have been invited.'"

"Yeah," I said. "Sometimes people do invite the immediate neighbors to outdoor parties."

"But in formal gowns?" she asked.

She was right—a formal party is usually not for the neighbors. I was prepared to leave it there, but as we climbed out of the SUV, a question occurred.

"Hey, how did you know it was their anniversary party?"

"Oh, they told me," Patti said. "I see them sometimes when they're walking the dog in the morning and I'm out waiting with Caitlin for the bus."

"Have they been over or anything since you've been ill?" I asked.

"No," said Patti.

"Do you think they know?"

"Yeah, I suppose they do," she said.

MOST of the other mall shoppers were mothers with preschool children, and older couples. Later that morning as we made our way through the mall, Patti remarked what a luxury it was to be able to shop in the morning, and recalled again how harried she'd been while working at the clinic. Her boss, she said, would sometimes let the office assistants clothes-shop for the radiologists. "We'd give them our credit cards and tell them what we had seen or were looking for, for our kids, and they'd go out and get the stuff. She wanted us in the office doing mammograms."

At GapKids, Patti was looking over summer dresses for her girls when she remembered that she left some clothes she needed to return in the SUV. I offered to get them, and she gave me her key chain. Walking toward the parking lot, I flipped through the plastic key tags attached to the chain: for the supermarket, the video store, and so on. The last was for Dick's Sporting Goods. That tag suddenly seemed a powerful symbol to me, connecting Patti DiNitto to her former neighbor down the street—Dick's was where Bob Wills purchased the gun he used to kill his wife.

Patti and Renan had never met, but I wondered if they had, if maybe they could have helped each other. Like Patti, Renan was a physician with two children, was isolated at home, and struggled with a difficult marriage. Perhaps the two, if they'd met, could have found a way to confide in and strengthen each other; maybe instead of Patti watching a TV news report of Renan's death that night, Renan and her children could have taken shelter in Patti's home, maybe in the very guest room where I had slept.

By 11:30, I noticed Patti's left leg was dragging a bit and suggested we stop for an early lunch.

At a café, we pushed our trays through a cafeteria line, and then found an open table. On one side of the table was a bench and on the other side, a chair. I asked Patti which she would prefer, and she chose the bench.

"Scott always had to have the bench," she said.

"Always?" I asked. "You're not exaggerating?"

"Oh, no," she said, "always."

She described him as obsessive-compulsive.

We started eating our salads.

"At this point in my life," said Patti, "I really don't care if I get married or not, but for him to hightail it out of there without discussing things—I think he was having flashbacks from his marriage."

It took me a moment to realize she was again discussing the breakup with Scott.

"I was totally shocked," she continued. "We went out to dinner and at first I didn't even know what he was talking about. I was totally confused. I mean, we'd gone out off and on for a year.

It takes him that long to figure out I'm not the one? I feel like I stuck through the yucky part of his divorce, and then . . ."

"You were just the transition?" I offered.

"I guess so," she said.

"I just couldn't believe it. I'd gotten back from San Francisco on Wednesday, then Friday he hinted at it, then Tuesday night was the big blow-off—and that's *after* I drove *his* daughter to school that day, and made them both dinner. At night I'm like, 'What's the matter with you?' He's like, 'I got to lay down for a minute.' Then he tells me he wants to spend more time with his kids or by himself with his dog—and eventually he's going to want to start dating other women."

"What did you say?" I asked.

"I was never really good at comebacks," she said. "It doesn't matter. What I say or do makes no difference."

Patti became quiet and stared hard at me, as if making sure she could trust me.

Then she said, "He said to me, 'I'll miss you when you die.'"

She began to cry. I reached over and held her arm. She was wearing a thick, wool sweater. "I said to him, 'What? Do you know something I don't?' It's like he wasn't going to see me anymore and he wanted to get that in. Isn't that weird?"

I didn't know what to say so I just held her arm tighter.

"I never used to think about dying before," she said, "but since he brought it up—I just feel like my days are numbered. I know other people look at me and think, 'Is she going to make it?'—but he called me his best friend."

Patti cried a little more.

She continued, "I just kept looking at him. I stared at him for like a minute and then he goes, 'Oh, maybe I'll be hit by a car tomorrow, you know, we never know.' And I thought, 'Oh, like that makes it all better!'" Patti cried silently.

I felt I needed to do something. "Let's talk about this," I said, still holding her arm. "Your cancer is in remission, right?"

She nodded.

"You take whatever meds you're supposed to?"

"Yeah."

"You fly to California every month for this trial of what may be a groundbreaking vaccine?"

"Yeah."

"So not only are you okay right now, you're doing everything possible to keep yourself well in the future."

"Yeah," she said. "Maybe his mother didn't teach him about what to say and what not to say."

That was charitable on Patti's part, I thought. To divert her attention a little and give her a chance to recover, I told her about an incident that had happened to me. It was just a few weeks after Marie left, and I was at a local carnival on the afternoon of the Fourth of July. All the people around me seemed to be happy couples with their kids. Just then, a friend came up, slapped me on the shoulder, and congratulated me on becoming what he called "Brighton's most eligible bachelor"— this, when at that moment I felt so terrible over the loss of my family.

"Why does this keep happening to me?" Patti pleaded.

I told Patti how much I admired all she had achieved: medical school, her practice, buying the house on her own, raising Caitlin and Sarah.

"Now it all seems for nothing," she said, "and the house is too big. I thought by this time maybe I'd have someone else living in it with me, but even with the girls it seems big and empty, and looks like it's going to stay that way."

She began to cry again.

"I feel like I let everyone down," she said. "Medicine just requires so much time and energy. I lived a crazy life trying to do it all. Now everything I worked so hard for is gone. Maybe it would have been better if I'd been an accountant like my father wanted. Just live a status quo life, under the radar. Just do my job and do it well. Maybe I'd have led a better life."

I reminded her of an earlier comment she'd made, about never having rebelled as a teenager. "But you know, in a way you did," I said. "You were the first in your family to go to college, you became a physician, you entered a cutting-edge field of medicine, then bought a big house in a beautiful but stuffy neighborhood . . ."

Patti laughed. "It is stuffy," she said. "I don't know what I was thinking. I just liked the house, and the street is so pretty."

There was something else I was curious about. The previous night, when she had cried briefly at Applebee's, she mentioned that maybe it was "for all the crying she hadn't done in college and med school." I wondered what she had meant by that. What crying hadn't she done?

"My father had died," she began, between bites of salad. "Everything seemed blunted after that. And then things got really hard in med school. I just shut it all out. I was afraid to cry in front of all these guys who are doctors. I didn't think they wanted women to show emotion so I just don't remember crying much. A lot of kids there were kids of doctors—they had someone with experience at home to bounce ideas off of. I had nobody. Now, looking back, it doesn't make any difference. I feel

I'm more self-assured. I think I have had experiences that have strengthened me."

"You mean experiences like with men?" I asked.

"Yeah," she said. "With men, work, health, divorce."

She stopped to take another bite of salad.

"But if I had the choice," she continued, "between all those strengthening experiences or a life of luxury, I'd take the life of luxury."

The check came. I said I'd pay, but Patti had already opened her purse and insisted on paying. Slowly, we made our way back through the mall, across the parking lot, and to her car. Patti was tired, and we didn't talk much, but I was thinking about Renan, and I was thinking about Patti, and I was thinking that, as neighbors, we might have a chance to do things better this time.

7

Motion Sickness

AT 3:45 a.m., I chewed a motion sickness tablet and went outside my house to wait. It was 20 degrees. Sandringham Road was quiet: no cars or people, just frost-covered lawns lit by streetlamps. I paced the driveway to keep warm. At 4:15, my cell phone rang.

"I slept through my alarm!" It was Brian Kenyon, the man who delivered our newspapers. "I'll be there in five minutes."

With a slight feeling of bravado—I'd managed to get up earlier than my newspaper carrier—I went inside to wait. Then a troubling thought occurred: Brian had warned me to take Dramamine because, as he put it, "The last three people who rode with me barfed," but if he were getting a late start, wouldn't he drive the route even faster?

His van sped into my driveway and I jumped in. "I took the Dramamine," I told him.

"You could consider that a smart move," he said, "especially as now we're really going to be hauling."

I had never met Brian—didn't even know his name until a few days earlier. All I knew was that early each morning, as my neighbors and I slept, he delivered our papers. Every day, he was the first person who came to our homes; by the nature of his work, he didn't have much direct contact with us, but I wondered, nevertheless, what his perceptions were of the neighborhood. I decided I'd like to ride the route with Brian, to see Sandringham Road from his perspective. When I called to ask if I could do that, he was both gracious and enthusiastic, and readily agreed.

Our first stop that morning was the distribution center where carriers came to pick up the papers. A dozen vehicles, mostly pickups and vans, were parked there, many with their engines running. Most of the drivers were men in their twenties and thirties; Brian was thirty-four. They all seemed to know each other. Through open windows, they yelled greetings and good-natured insults.

"Hey, watch it!" Brian shouted back. "I've got a customer with me. I'm getting some respect."

I waited in the van while he went to get the papers.

Brian was powerfully built: 6 feet tall, 230 pounds, with a thick neck and brawny arms. That morning, he wore a black ski cap pulled low over his short, blond hair. His boot laces were untied, evidence of how fast he'd left his house that morning after oversleeping.

The local paper, the *Democrat and Chronicle*, came in bundles of fifty. There were also loose copies of the *Wall Street Journal*, *USA Today*, and *Barron's*, and color inserts for Don Pablo's, a low-cost Mexican restaurant chain. "Like a lot of my customers on Sandringham are just waiting to eat at Don Pablo's," Brian joked. We spent fifteen minutes stuffing the papers into blue plastic

bags so they'd stay dry regardless of the weather. (I'd always valued these blue bags—not only did they serve their intended purpose, but they were also handy for picking up after my dog.)

We bagged different combinations: the *Democrat* alone,
Democrat and *Journal*, *Democrat* and *USA Today*. When the last
paper was bagged, Brian declared, "We're out of here!" and sped
out of the parking lot backward. A bracelet that said "I Love
You Dad" swung wildly from the rearview mirror, and I felt the
first tinge of nausea.

It had been about a year since Brian took over the Houston
Barnard route. His typical day, he told me, ran like this: Get up
at 3:45, deliver papers for an hour and a half, return home for
another hour's sleep, get up again at 7:30; wake the three kids
and, with his wife, get them off to school; go to his day job as
a sales rep for an industrial products firm while his wife works
part-time at a Hallmark store. At night, be back in bed between
8:30 and 11, depending on how tiring the day had been.

The newspaper company hired Brian as an independent contractor; money for the papers, gas, even the blue bags, came out
of his own pocket. The bags, he told me, cost a quarter of a cent
apiece. Including year-end tips, Brian said he cleared about $800
a month. At Christmas, most customers tipped around $25, but a
few gave $100. The route took Brian about 12 hours a week, so—
as I calculated—for getting up every day at 3:45 a.m., he made
about $17 an hour.

"If I didn't need the money and I could quit, I would," he told
me. "I'd like to get a normal night's sleep."

THE *Democrat and Chronicle*, the local paper that Brian and I
were delivering that morning, had for many years been the flag-

ship paper of Gannett Co., one of the nation's largest newspaper chains. That was because the company was based in Rochester where its founder, Frank E. Gannett, lived. In fact, Frank Gannett lived on Sandringham Road, across the street from me and just five houses down. His home, a 9,000-square-foot Tudor Revival set on two and a half acres, had eighteen rooms, English gardens, and a pool. I never met Frank Gannett—he died in 1957, the same year my family originally moved to Sandringham— but Lou Guzzetta did. "He'd walk around the neighborhood," recalled Lou, "and talk to you, and pat children on the head." Gannett's ambitions reached beyond journalism: in 1940 he sought the Republican nomination for president and received 34 votes on the first ballot at the Republican National Convention. After his death, his widow, Caroline Gannett, continued to live in the house. Every December she'd have spotlights trained on the roof to showcase a life-size plastic Santa climbing down the chimney.

Back when newspapers were delivered by boys and girls on bikes rather than adults in cars, I filled in a few times for a friend who had the morning route in our neighborhood. I stopped my bike at nearly every house on Sandringham—including the Gannett house—to deliver the paper. I remember wondering what the insides of all those houses looked like, and what the people in them were doing.

Caroline Gannett died in 1979. Ownership of the house has turned over two or three times since then, but among some neighbors it's still referred to as "the Gannett house."

BRIAN Kenyon's first stop on his route that morning was the Country Club of Rochester. That was the club where I'd watched

Deb O'Dell play paddle tennis. With his left hand, Brian tossed three papers out the window. The blue bags skidded over the snow and came to rest within inches of the front door of the clubhouse. "I throw football and baseball right-handed, but my finesse arm is my left," he said.

At a house down the street, he threw left-handed over the top of the van for another bull's-eye.

Customers appreciated his reliability, and probably also his aim. Recently, he told me, he'd received a postcard from one that said, "Please don't ever go on vacation again."

Brian was raised in a small town in western Massachusetts on a suburban cul-de-sac with seven houses. "Best place in America to grow up," he said. "My parents had the neighborhood pool. Every summer evening, everyone got together chatting, sharing coffee, the kids playing. That's what I wanted for my kids—but I don't have it."

For more than a decade, Brian had lived on a busy street in the suburb of East Rochester. "Besides the traffic," he said, "there aren't many families with children. Also, there've been issues with some of the neighbors."

What issues? I asked him.

"Just people not being respectful of each other," he said. "I finally decided, 'We can't live in this neighborhood'—so we don't. We live in the house, but we find our community elsewhere, in church and at friends' houses."

When I thought about it later, Brian's solution to his neighborhood problem seemed simple enough: he just dismissed the neighborhood as nonexistent and made his social connections elsewhere. It's an attitude I had heard from others, too. I guessed that worked well enough for Brian, since between his newspaper route and full-time sales job, he wasn't home much. But I wondered if that approach was as satisfying for his wife, who worked outside the house only part-time, or for his children.

On a street adjacent to Sandringham, Brian backed out of one driveway, crossed the street at an angle, backed into the next driveway, and then reversed the process. He avoided shifting gears as much as possible because it was "less abuse on the transmission." Maybe so, but—despite the Dramamine—I was growing increasingly nauseous. Then the van suddenly slid off the side of a driveway. As we headed into a gully, Brian yelled, "Oh, shit!" He steered expertly around two trees but there was a moment of fear—for me, certainly, and I think also for him—when it seemed the van might roll over. Brian kept his head, though. He drove through a backyard and out onto the other side of the street.

"That was a very cool move," I said, relieved.

"We're running so late," he said, "I can't stop to reflect on how cool that move was."

At 5:18 we reached the southern end of Sandringham. Brian stopped momentarily to check the route list. "It's hard to remember who's on and off vacation," he said. Fifteen or twenty of his customers are away at any one time, he estimated. "They take a lot of vacations," he said. "Many spend the winter in Florida."

As he scanned the list of addresses, I recalled a conversation with Brian just two days earlier. We'd met for lunch at a restaurant not far from Sandringham, and just after we'd sat down, Patti DiNitto walked in. She looked well that day and was by herself.

"Here comes one of your other customers right now," I said to Brian as Patti approached our table. I asked if he'd like me to introduce him, to "put a face with a name."

"To tell you the truth," he said, "I don't even put a name with an address. All I know are the addresses. I wouldn't recognize anyone's name on your street. Now if you introduced her as '75 Sandringham'—that's an address where the people had a stop on their paper for the last two weeks—I'd say, 'Welcome back. Did you have a good vacation?'"

"Well, this is 322 Sandringham and she is, in fact, just back from a nice vacation," I joked to Brian, and then introduced him to Patti by name. She told us the trip to Arizona had worked out well; her daughter Caitlin's leg had only been sprained and had healed enough for her to enjoy most of the outdoor activities on the trip.

I didn't mention Patti's illness to Brian.

In the van, when he had finished noting who was out of town, Brian turned to me.

"Ready?" he asked.

He had told me earlier that on a normal day, depending on road conditions, delivering papers to all thirty-six houses on Sandringham took on average just six minutes. That would be six houses a minute or one every ten seconds. I felt sick enough already but was determined to stick it out at least to the end of the street.

"Ready," I said.

THE last time our neighborhood was prominently featured in the *Democrat and Chronicle* was on the occasion of the murder of Renan Wills. The paper played the story big: front page headline, A MARRIAGE ENDS IN VIOLENCE; photo of the Willses' house; photo of Bob Wills; photo of Renan Wills; map of Brighton showing the location of Sandringham Road.

That's about the most attention our neighborhood ever

received. On occasion, there have been other pieces: a doctor discusses a new medical study, a business executive comments on his company's earnings report. But though the paper might write *about* people in the neighborhood, it never could do much to promote a *sense* of neighborhood. For one thing, as a publication covering all of Rochester, it was too diverse to examine closely what might be going on in any single neighborhood, let alone on any one street. Moreover, by its nature, the paper offered only one-way communication: editors and reporters talking to readers, not readers talking to each other (exceptions being Letters to the Editor and guest essays). In short, the paper Brian and I were delivering that morning was largely irrelevant to the question of how residents of a neighborhood connect or don't connect to each other.

The Internet, however, held real promise.

From its earliest days, sociologists and social psychologists debated whether the Internet might strengthen or weaken neighborhood relationships. In early studies, they wired parts of neighborhoods for Internet access—leaving other parts unwired—then tried to compare over time the relative strength of contacts between residents who had access to each other and those who did not. Results were mixed. Now, after decades of experience, the answer still remains unclear, or perhaps the answer is Yes: the Internet can *strengthen* relations among neighbors and it can *weaken* relations; it all depends on how it's used.

On the "weaken" side, the concern has always been that, because there are only so many hours in a day, time spent on the Internet with distant, online friends will necessarily reduce time spent in real, face-to-face relations. A poignant example was offered by a woman in Tennessee who wrote me: "My late husband became a member of a couple of online communities a few years ago. They gradually became his circle of friends. He isolated himself from real-time friends and neighbors because he had friends online. So far, okay. *But*, he had a heart attack, then another, and where was his community? Nowhere, everywhere, but not here. Not where they could offer any support or help. I was not even able to find how to access the groups to let them know he died."

Similarly, a woman in Texas wrote: "The reason that proximity should be a reason for acquaintance is that the person in California you're online with is not going to pick your child up from soccer or baby sit while you're in chemo."

On the other hand, the Internet can enhance neighbor-to-neighbor communication in a way that no other media—including the daily newspaper—can. Already, thanks to some early innovators, thousands of people across the country use online services designed to help neighbors connect.

Jared Nissim, thirty-five, was raised in Westchester, New York. As a child, he lived for a while on an Israeli kibbutz and found he liked the sense there of a close community. Later, back in Manhattan and living in an apartment, he felt isolated. "I wanted to meet the other people who lived in my building," he recalled. "I was tired of passing them in the hallway, only to exchange a nod but never actually getting to know them."

Nissim slipped a note under everyone's door. "Hi, my name is Jared, in #100," it said, and then asked for their e-mails and said he'd "organize something." More than half responded positively. "I had a hunch that turned out to be true," he recalled. "Most of the people who lived in my building wanted to meet each other—they just needed a good opportunity and reason to do so." What Nissim eventually "organized" was MeetTheNeighbors.org.

Meet the Neighbors serves all kinds of neighborhoods, but as suggested by its welcome page—which resembles a multi-story building—it's mostly aimed at apartment dwellers in big cities. "Our whole point is to connect people who are already physically next to each other," Nissim told me. "People in apartment buildings can go years without getting to know even the people on the other side of the wall."

The phenomenon is well known. One young man wrote me: "I live in a 23-floor building in Manhattan and, incredibly enough, I don't know the first name of one single one of my neighbors. Maybe this is my mistake adapting to the surroundings, instead of trying to do things the way I learnt growing up in another country where knowing your neighbors is part of daily life."

Residents of a building who register with Meet the Neighbors can communicate through a message board, post information about neighborhood services and events, and vote on building-wide issues. They can also send private messages to each other, if they both choose.

By 2009, more than 2,500 buildings and nearly 14,000 residents had registered.

With Nissim's permission, I looked in on the company's website for a registered, twelve-story apartment building in Brooklyn. On the message board, an exchange about plumbing began, "This may be a little personal, but is anyone else having issues with their toilets? Mine flushes very slowly . . ." Other message threads concerned problems with the building's heat, and complaints about the slowness of repairs.

Nissim wasn't surprised by the nature of the postings. "The first level of communication between neighbors often is complaining about issues of the building," he said. "There's a pent-up frustration that gets released that way. When the neighbors finally get together about these issues, then you see a shift to more normal transactions—someone's got a washer/dryer for sale, someone recommends a nearby hardware store or restaurant."

I also saw a different kind of posting:

From a resident who was an art student: "Hello neighbors—Hope you can make it to my show—the opening is saturday 6-8 and will be up through january 12."

Nissim commented, "Eventually, the neighbor-to-neighbor conversations build into real social interaction: friendships evolve, love relations evolve. When you remove the barriers that keep people from speaking, who knows what else will develop?"

Sometimes what develops is just tolerance. After getting to know some of the people in her Washington, DC, building, a woman wrote me: "[W]hen I come home to hear music through my walls (now), I don't get angry. I just think that my neighbor, whom I now know personally, will certainly turn down the music in a bit so as not to disturb me, and he always does, because of course, he knows me personally, too."

A similar online service, though one that does not generally serve high-rise apartment buildings, is i-Neighbors.org. Users of i-Neighbors, according to director Keith Hampton, a sociologist at the Annenberg School for Communication at the University of Pennsylvania, generally reside in three areas: new suburban developments, established suburban developments, and the "20% most disadvantaged neighborhoods in America, which are mostly inner-city communities." Founded in 2004, the nonprofit site, now active throughout the United States and Canada, aims to "create neighborhoods that are safer, better informed, more trusting, and better equipped to deal with local issues." The service operates as an ongoing experiment in community building by a team of faculty and students directed by Hampton.

"People have the perception that something is wrong today in the places they live," says Hampton, "that their community is lost, and they are intent on trying to find it. Interestingly, the tendency is to blame technology for the loss, and to use technology to repair it."

I-Neighbors allows residents to post photos, restaurant reviews, and messages, but the most used and most useful feature, says Hampton, is the e-mail list. "People will only regularly check so many websites," he explains, "but if you log on to your computer and an e-mail from a neighbor comes right into your regular e-mail, it has an impact."

"On the other hand," he continued, "some homeowner associations—such as condos and town houses—want to control communication among neighbors." He said homeowner associations actually had threatened i-Neighbors with lawsuits to try to prevent its members from using the service to communicate with each other. "They have rules against putting flyers and letters under neighbors' doors," said Hampton, "and they've tried to stop us from enabling neighbors to communicate with each other without the association's approval."

Hampton's own neighborhood backs up to a wooded area. "There was concern about people hunting deer and firing guns near homes. It was an issue the neighbors could communicate about using the e-mail list," he said.

In some areas, issues are even more serious. "There are neighborhoods in great distress as a result of crime, where neighbors use i-Neighbors literally to protect themselves," he explained. "These are inner-city communities that face gang and drug activity. They are among some of the most active users of the site, using it to organize, help each other, and provide support to look out for and care for each other's home and well-being."

"I can tell you something about your neighbors," Brian Kenyon, my newspaper deliveryman, said. "They expect and appreciate and reward good service. They have set desires, but they're also very understanding people. At times, I've lost my bearings and veered onto lawns."

Brian said this as he drove forward into 375 Sandringham, across to 370, forward into 350, then back and then forward again into 340 and back into 296. I needed air. I rolled down the window and unzipped my coat. As I tried some deep breathing, Brian continued his commentary on the culture of my street; unless I was mistaken, he seemed to take a perverse pleasure in calmly lecturing me as I hung my face out the window, gasping for air.

"One lawn had just been reseeded," he continued. "I called the guy and apologized and he said, 'Don't worry about it. We'll take care of it.' When people speak of a neighborhood of affluence, they expect people to be cocky or power-tripping. I have yet to find that. While they may have money, I have found people have matured beyond cockiness."

By the time we backed out of 290—the O'Dells' driveway—and across Sandringham and backward into the next driveway, I was sweating and didn't really care what Brian thought of my neighbors. I only wanted to complete the van ride without embarrassing myself. I tried keeping my head down near my knees, a tactic that, ironically, caused me to miss seeing Brian toss the paper at the front door of my own house. At Lou Guzzetta's, I looked up briefly to see his paper land at the side door.

"I would love to live in a picture-perfect neighborhood like this someday," Brian continued. "Will I ever obtain the money to do it? I don't know. I'll never do it the way some people have done it. I'll never get a medical degree or go to law school."

Could he not see how sick I was? He just kept talking.

We were near the Willses' house. The end of the ride was in sight.

"There was a murder . . . in this house," I said to Brian. Speaking in short bursts felt like it might keep me from vomiting. "Guy killed his wife. Then himself. Kids were home."

Brian said he remembered it. "I don't think I could live in a house where a murder occurred. I didn't realize this was the house."

Brian took me halfway back up the street and dropped me off at my house. I picked up the newspaper from the front step. As I slipped it from the blue bag and unrolled it, out fell the insert for Don Pablo's Mexican restaurant: CREATE YOUR OWN LUNCH COMBO $8.49 SPICY GROUND BEEF, PORK, CHEESE OR CHICKEN TACOS!

I raced for the john.

8

A Father Ten Feet Tall

WE took Sunday evening family supper in a small room on the back of the house, seated around a simple wooden table: Bill Fricke, at the head; his wife, Susan; thirteen-year-old Allison, eleven-year-old Jonathan, and me. On the floor nearby lay Pumpkin, their Duck Tolling Nova Scotia Retriever. We helped ourselves family-style to a casserole of white rice and veggies.

Jonathan, whom they called "Bubba," started the conversation. A friend's mom, he said, had just been made Eastman Kodak's chief of sales in the Far East. The whole family would be moving to Hong Kong for two years.

In his measured, deep, flat Midwestern voice, Bill said to me, "You see, that's what I mean by 'boring.' We would never be able to do that."

In interviews preceding my sleepover, Bill had repeatedly described his life as boring: work was boring, Rochester was boring, the routine of family life was boring. I wasn't sure if he really meant it or was just being self-deprecating.

"Living in another country for six months or a year—now that would be interesting," he said.

Bill Fricke, fifty-four, stood over six feet tall. He was lean and muscular, with short graying hair and a long, craggy face. Even before I learned he was born in central Illinois, it occurred to me that—given both his build and slightly melancholic bearing—if you put Bill in a dark suit and top hat, the president he would most resemble would be Abraham Lincoln.

I asked Bill and Susan—they are both physicians—if they might spice up their lives by volunteering overseas with a group such as Doctors Without Borders.

"Yeah, well, I think they're looking for primary care docs . . ." said Bill.

Bill was a pathologist and Susan a pediatrician specializing in autism.

"Not a lot of autistic refugees?" I asked.

"Yeah," agreed Susan. "And a pathologist? I don't think so."

Susan asked, "So how's the book coming?" She spoke with traces of a New York accent. To Allison and Bubba, she added, "Remember, I explained Mr. Lovenheim is writing a book about the neighborhood?" The children nodded dutifully.

I said it was coming along okay, and she asked whom else in the neighborhood I had interviewed. This was a question I was frequently asked by neighbors, and I always made sure to answer it honestly while still maintaining the trust of everyone who had opened up to me. I told Susan I'd interviewed Lou Guzzetta, Deb and Dave O'Dell, Jamie Columbus, Patti Di-Nitto, and some family members and friends of Renan Wills. She didn't know the O'Dells or Patti, and hadn't known Renan, but said she had run into Lou on the street once or twice while walking the dog.

"Is it legal to ask what Lou Guzzetta's like?" she asked. "Someone his age must have good stories about the neighborhood." She added, "Do you remember him, Allison? We met him once walking the dogs."

Responding to Susan's question—Is it legal to ask what Lou Guzzetta's like?—was tricky. I was, after all, a guest in her home and it would have been courteous to answer. But neighbors frequently asked me about each other, and often the questions were more pointed: Does so-and-so work outside the house? Who's that man I see going in and out every day? Did you hear anything about their family's business being in trouble? I didn't want to violate confidences, and I was sure being seen as loose-lipped would discourage people from talking to me, so whenever I was asked what I'd learned about a neighbor, I always demurred, as I did that evening with Susan.

"Yes, Lou has some interesting stories," I said to Susan, and hoped that she wouldn't think me impolite for not saying more.

The rest of the talk at dinner mostly concerned the children's activities. Allison, an eighth grader, was in rehearsals for the school musical. Bubba, in sixth grade, was preparing for a presentation on Pablo Picasso the next morning. He'd made a papier-mâché figure of the artist and had a clever plan for presenting his report.

Bill rose from the table, towering over his family and me, and went into the kitchen. A moment later, he returned carrying a fruit pie. Over dessert, the talk turned to plans for the next day. Allison would have chores to do before school, and after school would go to play rehearsal until 9:30. Bubba would have guitar and trumpet lessons, then ski club until 10. Susan would pack the children lunch as well as dinner.

At 7:30 sharp, Bill announced dinner was over and that it was time for homework.

"Who needs help?" asked Susan.

"I do, with physics," said Allison. She was pretty, slender like her father but petite like her mom, with a quiet, almost whispery voice. Eighth-grade midterms were tomorrow. "I just don't understand it," she said.

Everyone helped clear the table, then Bubba went upstairs to work on Picasso while Bill, Susan, and I stayed in the kitchen.

I'm sure the Frickes weren't always the ideal family, but that evening—whether for my sake or not—they offered a good approximation of it. Their quiet, seemingly stable domesticity looked just fine to me, particularly since my own family had fallen apart. Parents at home on a Sunday evening with their kids? What a concept. Eating dinner, doing dishes, helping with homework? Bill Fricke was right—it was boring, but it was the most precious boring I could imagine, and I drank in every mundane detail.

BILL Fricke hadn't originally been on my short list for next neighbor to get to know. When a mutual friend introduced me to him some years earlier, Bill had struck me as quiet, even a little gloomy. But I was looking for a married couple with children—and I wanted to focus on the husband to balance my recent attention to Deb O'Dell, Jamie Columbus, and Patti DiNitto—so I couldn't rule out Bill and his family. Still, I remembered those three neighbors who had rejected my requests. Though with thirty-six houses on the street there were plenty of neighbors left to meet, the number with children living at home was limited. I couldn't afford to lose too many more, so with Bill, I was cautious.

A common element of the three rejections, I realized, was that when I told my neighbors what I wanted to do, I had been inside their homes, or in one case, in front of their home on the driveway. Maybe asking permission to step inside people's lives while actually inside their homes reminded them too easily of the privacy they were being asked to give up. Therefore, I decided with Bill to stay away from his house as long as possible.

I arranged an initial meeting with Bill at Starbucks on a weekday evening. He wore an old sweatshirt and jeans. He said he wasn't a coffee drinker and had rarely been to Starbucks. While he sipped a decaf iced tea, I sketched out my interest in exploring how we live as neighbors today. Almost immediately, Bill spoke of his own sense of isolation. "We live as strangers to each other," he said.

I hadn't spent enough time with Bill yet to appreciate how this sentiment—his sense of living among strangers—was a rare source of discontentment within an otherwise contented life. It might be what the writer John Keats, in his antisuburbia novel of 1956, called "a crack in the picture window." I wanted to explore the issue further with him, but not just yet—we still needed some time to get to know each other.

I asked Bill if he'd do me the favor of allowing me to interview him about his background and his experience of living on Sandringham Road, and maybe later chronicle a typical day in his life. He agreed, and encouraged me to talk to Susan, as well. He asked if I'd use real names and I said I would like to. "Well," he said, "you're using your own real name. I guess it's okay if you use mine. I mean, you're not going to alienate the people you're living among."

My interviews with Bill began that evening at Starbucks and continued over three or four sessions in several other coffee shops. It wasn't until four months later that I even entered his house, and that was to interview Susan. Later, I pointed out that chronicling a day in Bill's life—which by then I knew began at 6 a.m.—would be easier if I could stay over the night before. He and Susan both agreed, but Bill warned me, of course, that sleeping over would be "boring."

BY Sandringham standards, the Frickes' kitchen was modest, with limited counter space. That Sunday evening after dinner, Susan, just 5 foot 2—a foot shorter than Bill—stood at the sink and loaded the dishwasher. Behind her, Pumpkin sat waiting for scraps. Bill stood bent over a counter where Allison was studying physics.

Between cleaning the dishes and helping with homework, Bill and Susan coordinated the next day's schedule. Who would pick up Allison and Bubba after school and again after evening activities, who would shop for groceries, who would prepare dinner? Though the next day was Monday, it was not one of the two Mondays a month when, in the evening, Bubba had Boy Scout meetings or campouts. Bill always went with him. "I think it's important for fathers to do these things with a child," he told me earlier.

Susan, finished with the dishes, began preparing Bubba's and Allison's meals for the next day. As we chatted, I noted her use of Yiddish terms: Bubba was "boychik," the dog's stuffed toy was a "shmata."

Bubba popped in to ask if he could watch *The Simpsons*. Earlier, Bill had told me the family seldom watched TV—they didn't get cable and one of their sets was an old black-and-white. But *The Simpsons* and some news shows were occasional exceptions to the rule, and Susan told Bubba if all his homework was done, he could watch.

At some point, I became aware that Bill was not around.

"He's in the garage," said Susan, "washing the cars."

"Washing the cars?"

It was seven degrees out—I knew that because I'd checked earlier that evening before I left my house to walk to the Frickes'. I opened the door to the attached garage and what I saw surprised me: there was Bill, in black rubber boots and gloves, sloshing soapy water from a bucket over Susan's minivan and his Toyota Camry. I watched as he scrubbed the cars with a long-handled black brush and then rinsed them with a garden hose.

It had not occurred to me that any resident of my street—let alone a physician—would be out in his garage on a frigid night washing cars. Bill told me he washed the cars at least weekly during the winter because road salt builds up. "You can see we're not into fancy cars," he said, "but they're a big expense, and if it helps to keep them running so we can get another year out of them, I figure it saves twenty thousand dollars. Plus, I suppose they just look better."

I could see Bill's point about road salt, but I didn't quite buy that washing the cars by hand was mostly about money. After all, this was a family with two physicians' salaries, and though I didn't know Bill and Susan's income, I was pretty sure they could afford to go to a car wash if they wanted and get "the works"— including undercarriage salt removal—whenever they wished. I suspected Bill's choice to hand-wash the cars was about his own sense of frugality and the value of physical labor, and to demonstrate those values to his children. Probably for the same reason, Bill cut his own grass and cleared the snow from the sidewalks on both sides of their corner lot. (The Frickes were often the only residents of Sandringham, including me, who in the winter regularly kept their sidewalks clear.) That probably also explained why the radio on the kitchen counter was an old GE table-top in a brown leather case and not a BOSE, why the refrigerator was not a Sub-Zero, and why the mushrooms in the dinner casserole came from a second freezer in the basement where Susan stored vegetables she bought in bulk.

Fortunately for me, Bill's frugality did not extend to the comfort of his guests. I would be sleeping that night in the maid's room over the garage—like Patti DiNitto's, the Frickes' home was built before the Depression, when maids' rooms were a common feature of houses on Sandringham. As he finished rinsing the Camry, Bill said that, while he usually kept the heat off in the garage, earlier that afternoon, for my benefit, he had turned it on. "Your room is right above here," he said, gesturing toward the ceiling, "and there's no insulation in the floor. So I figured if I turn the heat on, it might keep your room a little warmer tonight."

WHEN he finished in the garage, Bill washed his hands and said he'd be going to the living room to read. "You can sit in any chair in there you like," he said, "except the yellow one."

The Frickes' home sat at the east end of Sandringham, at the opposite end of the street from me, just across and a few doors down from where Bob and Renan Wills had lived. Their house, a 1926 Tudor Revival, was one of the first built in the Houston Barnard Tract. It had a steeply pitched slate roof with overlapping gables, leaded casement windows, and two massive chimneys. The outside was covered in stucco and decorative half-timbering.

Inside, among nearly 4,500 square feet of living space, were many handsomely furnished rooms. My favorite was the living room. Bill and Susan had made a hobby of learning about Chinese antiques and had filled the room with Oriental rugs and antique Chinese furniture, including a writing desk from the Qing dynasty, a pair of children's chairs, and a tray table that Bill said was designed as an "opium table." But the most eye-catching item to me was a gleaming, ebony, Austrian-made Bösendorfer grand piano. "It was the last piano made with real ivory keys," said Bill. "We had mixed emotions about it because of that, but it's a richer sound than Steinway."

I would have liked that evening to ask Bill to play, but Susan had warned against it. "Bill's a very good musician," she told me earlier, "but he'll never play for you, so don't ask."

Bill took what was clearly "Dad's chair": a large, yellow wing-back armchair with ball and claw feet and sculpted wooden legs. He said it was a Chippendale reproduction in the Colonial-Revival style, probably made in the 1920s, and that he'd bought it at a flea market for $10 and had it recovered. Propping his slippered feet onto the "opium table," which he used as a foot stool, Bill turned on a floor lamp and began reading an article entitled "Protein Electrophoresis in Clinical Diagnosis," from a science journal.

I needed something to do while Bill read. There was a magazine rack next to the sofa on which I was seated with back copies of *Oriental Furniture*. I picked one up and had just begun an article when Susan joined us, taking a seat at the other end of the sofa, and settling in with some sewing.

*   *   *

WILLIAM Fricke, born in 1949, grew up in the central Illinois town of Jacksonville, population 20,000. His father was a physician and his mother a social worker. "Life was slow and simple and easy," he told me earlier. Bill rode his bike to school every day. He was a Boy Scout. He mowed lawns, shoveled snow, and delivered newspapers. For field trips, his class would go to nearby New Salem to see the log houses where Abraham Lincoln lived and worked as a young man, and to Springfield, to view the Lincoln family home. On weekends, "Mom would make us lunch and we'd ride our bikes downtown to a movie or just ride out of town for a couple of miles." In the summer, Bill's parents took him and his older sister on car trips, often lasting a month. By the time he was through junior high school, he'd seen most of the country.

At Washington University in Saint Louis, Bill majored in music history and played classical piano. If you looked at his hands, you could easily imagine him as a pianist: they were large, with long, slender fingers. After graduation, he was unsure what to do and traveled around Europe while trying to figure it out. Returning to Jacksonville, Bill got a job as a technician at a local hospital, found he liked it, and went back to Washington University for medical school, but again without much direction. "I was at my wit's end as to what I was going to specialize in and tried literally everything," he recalled. A project in the tissue-typing laboratory did the trick: "It turns out I'm interested in how things work—the inner workings of things," he said, explaining his eventual focus on pathology. "Patho-physiology looks at the basic mechanism of disease. How does blood clot? How do wounds heal? How does the immune system work?"

Bill did a residency in pathology at Chapel Hill, North Carolina. His time there was "uneventful—like most of my life," except that he met another resident, a petite, energetic, smart Jewish girl from suburban New York City. He and Susan Hyman were introduced at a party by a mutual friend. "I don't remember much about it except that I liked her from the moment we met," he recalled. When they told their families they were serious about each other, Susan's father was not pleased. "Susan was afraid her father would disown her," recalled Bill. The issue was that Bill was not Jewish. "I was raised as a liberal Christian," he said, "but my mother and I didn't believe any of it. I'm basically a heretic." When Bill agreed to raise the couple's children Jewish and give them a Jewish education at least through Bar Mitzvah, Susan's father withdrew his objection.

Early in their marriage, Bill and Susan settled in Columbia, Maryland, so that Susan could work in pediatrics at Johns Hopkins University. Allison and Bubba were born there. "We nicknamed him 'Bubba,'" Susan explained earlier, "because he was conceived in North Carolina and everyone there is called 'Bubba.'" Bill worked for the National Institutes of Health in a blood-banking fellowship, but eventually tired of the job. "After nearly eight years, I woke up one day and just couldn't fill out another government form," he told me earlier. That's when he found a job in pathology in Rochester.

Susan, reluctant to leave Maryland, nevertheless was offered a job in her specialty—pediatric autism—at Rochester's largest hospital and agreed to move. Unlike her husband, she had had no uncertainty about her career. Since high school, Susan had known she wanted to be a doctor. At Brown University, she did a combined undergraduate and medical school program, then a residency at Chapel Hill. A main interest all along was what she termed "the biology of behavior." Now, as a developmental pediatrician, she assessed and treated children with neurological handicaps. Recently, she and colleagues patented a gene they believe is related to autism.

Now, Bill was Associate Director of Pathology and Laboratory Medicine at Rochester General Hospital. He supervised four assistants and, through them, a staff of nearly a hundred technicians. Through his lab, he estimated, passed the blood samples and tissue biopsies of nearly 40 percent of the population of Rochester. Much of Bill's workday involved examining blood and tissue samples under a microscope to detect infections, cancer, or other diseases. I once asked him if I could visit at the lab but he tried to dissuade me. "It would be boring," he said. "There'd be nothing interesting to see." When I protested that he dealt with issues of life and death, and expressed my admiration for the importance of his work, he turned aside the compliment. "Susan's the real star," he said. "I'm just some hack at a hospital."

At nine o'clock that evening, without saying a word, Bill put down his science journal and went to the piano. He began with scales, then chord progressions. Susan raised both eyebrows at me as if to say, "This is a surprise!" She put down her sewing to listen.

"Oy," said Bill as he stumbled on a passage.

Bill's playing lasted about twenty minutes and included portions of a Brahms intermezzo and Bach's "Well-Tempered Klavier."

When he was done, I complimented his playing.

"Thanks. I stink," he said, and sat down again to read in his yellow, wingback chair.

In a stage whisper, Susan said to me, "I've never heard him play for anyone but his mother."

Bill read some more and Susan sewed some more, and then

around a quarter to ten, Bill said it was about time for bed, and Susan agreed. As we all left the living room together, I asked Bill about the origin of the Oriental rugs. The two larger ones were made in Iran, he explained, and the smaller ones in the Caucuses. He said he would like to get one large rug for the whole room. "I would love to go to Iran," he said. "I saw a trip to northern Iran advertised in—"

"You don't have enough life insurance to go to Iran," Susan interrupted, adding to me, "That's not anywhere he's going anytime soon."

EVEN with the heat in the garage turned on, the Frickes' maid's room was freezing and I had to use both an electric space heater and an electric blanket to keep warm. It was nicely furnished, though. There was an Oriental rug, and a brass bed that came from Bill's uncle's farm in Missouri. Before I climbed into bed, I peeked out a small window that looked onto Sandringham. Across the road, past the glare of the streetlamp, I could see the front of the redbrick Colonial house that had been Bob and Renan Willis's home.

Bill Fricke—not a big TV watcher—said he hadn't learned about the murder until the next morning. "I didn't know a thing about it," he had told me. "Next day, I went jogging and saw a reporter standing there. I couldn't believe it." Bill said he had known Renan only casually. "I had talked to her a couple of times about patients, but I didn't know her well. I think I heard her husband bounced around to a couple of different jobs— clearly he had problems."

Susan, who often stayed up later than Bill, had seen police cars on the street the night of the murder but thought some teens might be having a party and that someone had complained. She remembered, "Then at six a.m., a friend called in a panic. She'd heard on the radio that a doctor couple with two young children on Sandringham were killed. She was afraid it was us. The next morning, I told the kids when they left for school that something bad had happened and that Emily's mommy and daddy were dead but that Emily and her brother were safe. It was awful. Bubba was seven and was very scared."

Long ago, the Frickes' house had itself been touched by violence. In December 1971, around 11:30 at night, dynamite exploded near the back of the house—near the room where the Frickes and I had had Sunday dinner. A judge and his wife and their teenage son who lived there then were home, but escaped injury. Police made plaster casts of footprints outside the house, sent bomb fragments to an FBI laboratory in Washington, and tapped the phones of several local felons over whose convictions the judge had presided. The next day, police went up and down Sandringham interviewing neighbors to see if anyone had noticed anything suspicious. Many said they had heard the explosion, but none had anything useful to report. The only person who saw something was a fourteen-year-old newsboy, who had noticed a red Mustang parked on the street and a man standing outside what later would be the Frickes' house. The boy told police what he'd seen, but nothing ever came of it.

As I looked out the window of the maid's room that night, I thought of the newsboy and what he saw all those years ago—and I couldn't help but think of Renan Wills, who had lived across the street. Two homes facing each other, touched by violence a generation apart; one incident benign and the other deadly; one where no one was hurt and one where no one wasn't.

I made my nightly call to Marla. She said she missed me and

asked how the evening had gone. I told her about Bill washing the cars by hand and playing piano. An amateur musician herself, she was impressed to hear of the Bösendorfer and the pieces Bill had played. I didn't mention how being at the Frickes made me miss having an intact family—I didn't think she'd want to hear about that. We said we loved each other and wished each other good night. Then I climbed into the brass bed, crawled under the covers, and slept.

AT a few minutes past 6:00 a.m., thirteen-year-old Allison Fricke came down to breakfast in her pajamas and robe. Sleepy-eyed, she held a teddy bear in one arm. She went to the basement and a minute later came back with frozen waffles and put them in the toaster oven. Bubba entered the kitchen next, followed by his father.

Bill wore a T-shirt and running shorts; his hair was tousled, and he looked pale. He turned on the old GE kitchen radio to NPR and began cooking egg whites for the kids; at the same time, he emptied the dishwasher. On the radio, the local NPR station gave the forecast: harsh winds and temperatures in the teens.

By 6:30, the kids were fed and Bill was ready to exercise, but then, realizing he hadn't heard anything yet from Susan, said, "I better make sure she's awake," and went back upstairs. A couple minutes later he returned and I went with him into the basement, where he immediately began riding an exercise bike with two-pound weights strapped to his ankles. "This is easier than riding outside on a day like today," he said. "I bought this bike for sixty dollars used." The previous summer, Bill competed in an AARP-sponsored triathlon, and he planned to do another this year if his hip was okay; he'd been having some problems with bursitis.

There wasn't much for me to do while Bill exercised. Unlike Lou Guzzetta, who had exhorted me to "get in shape" while he worked out at the Y, Bill seemed content to let me watch and ask questions. We listened on NPR to a segment about Senator Joseph Lieberman's presidential campaign. "I really don't like these religious types," Bill said. "They tend to be dangerous. Only Carter turned out to be okay." Though he and Susan were giving their children a Jewish education, Bill remained a skeptic. "I don't believe any of it," he told me earlier. "You know in the synagogue, that glass wall in front that looks out onto those big trees?" he asked. I knew the wall he meant because the Frickes and I belonged to the same Reform synagogue. "Once I heard the rabbi stand up there and say, 'This is God's sanctuary,' but I thought, 'No, outside is God's sanctuary. This is just a building made by people.'"

Bill lay down on a floor mat—it said MARIE FRICKE and had belonged to his mother—and began doing sit-ups. Then he stood again to do arm curls with orange hand weights. At 6:50, his exercise done, Bill went upstairs to shower and dress.

I returned to the kitchen just as Susan came in, dressed for work. "Good morning," she said. "I have three minutes to get out of here," and rushed back upstairs to get something she'd forgotten.

That intensity was more like the Susan I'd come to know on earlier visits than the woman I'd seen the previous night calmly sewing in the living room. In one earlier interview, Susan had sat in a straight-backed chair. As she answered my questions, she rocked back and forth with her hands tucked under her legs as if trying to contain her energy. And that was on her day off.

That morning, she was scheduled to see patients in the hospital. In the afternoon, she would drive to several outlying counties to consult with school staff. "They have six- or seven-year-olds," she told me, "possibly with reactive attachment disorder—it's like a junior version of post-traumatic stress syndrome. These kids have experienced fetal alcohol syndrome, foster homes, witnessed all kinds of violence. Now the school's looking for help and wants to know if the kids are autistic."

The daily demands of work and her desire to be present and active with her family required Susan to work long hours and do everything efficiently. Four days a week she was at the hospital—two seeing patients and two doing research. On Fridays, her day off—between frequent calls and pages from colleagues—she took care of the house. "I don't have a cleaning lady," she told me with evident pride. "I try to get all the housekeeping, laundry, errands, and food shopping done on my day off so we can have better family time on the weekends." Once, on a Friday, I had happened to see her coming home from the supermarket. The back of her van was completely filled with groceries and it was only 7:30 a.m.

Susan and Bill had hired a nanny to watch their children after school until they got home from work, usually around 6 p.m. The first one home would make dinner. "I try to make a 'do-ahead' dinner like lasagna or stew so it can be microwaved," Susan told me. "Then it's homework—the kids still require attention. Between seven and nine p.m. or so, it's all about them. After they're in bed, I do my charting, dictate reports, and review abstracts and journal articles." She usually worked until 1 a.m. Fortunately, she could get by on five or six hours' sleep a night, and getting to sleep was not a problem. "I can turn it right off," she said, a skill she learned through hypnosis.

"When it comes right down to it," she told me, "Bill and I are just working parents. Yes, we're blessed with these great jobs, but otherwise we schlep and chauffer the same as everyone else. I get up and get the kids off. I do everything normal mothers do. I just do it in less time."

At 7:02, Susan shepherded Allison and Bubba into the garage; each carried backpacks that contained their lunch as well as dinner. Bubba also carried a grocery bag with a papier-mâché bust of Pablo Picasso. "You saw it," Susan called back to me as she got into the car, "the 'tornado' of how this family gets out in the morning!"

WHEN Bill returned to the kitchen, showered and dressed for work, he fixed hot oatmeal and half a grapefruit for our breakfast. As we ate, at the same simple wooden table at which we'd had dinner the night before, we chatted about the stock market, inflated CEO salaries, and other news of the day.

Before leaving for work, Bill had one more chore to do. "The piano goes out of tune unless we keep the air humidified," he explained as he filled a bucket of water and carried it to a spot near the living room.

BILL'S route to work that morning took him down Sandringham Road. "Maybe it's my small-town background," he said, "but I miss driving down a street in the morning as opposed to a highway. A street is a more personal experience."

Small-town life had its benefits, Bill offered. "In a little town, people can be controlling, snoopy, and there's an incredible lack of privacy. On the other hand, they are your friends when you're sick. When you get a little dowdy in your old age, that's where your support comes from. One of the tragedies of modern life is that kind of network becomes very hard to maintain. Instead, we live too much as strangers to each other."

That was the second time Bill had used that phrase—"live as strangers to each other"—with me, and this time I had to ask him about it.

I pointed out various houses on Sandringham: "Do you know them?" I asked. "How about them?" His reply was nearly always no. Perhaps that's why, I thought, the list of emergency contact numbers taped to the Frickes' refrigerator—with multiple numbers each for Bill, Susan, and the nanny—included no neighbors. What few neighbors he knew, Bill said, were dog owners whom he'd met while walking Pumpkin. "Without a dog, you could live next to someone for years and never know who they are."

It made me wonder how the Frickes had ended up in the neighborhood. Susan had told me that when she and Bill moved to Rochester, their real estate agent showed them Sandringham right away. "The agent said, 'Oh, two doctors, you've got to look at the Houston Barnard neighborhood,'" she recalled.

"The truth is," said Bill, "people live in this neighborhood for a variety of reasons. Some think it's 'the place' to live. I've met people who say they never thought they'd live on Sandringham—that is, they're so pleased they've 'made it—they've arrived.' For us, though," he continued, "we just liked it because it has trees, sidewalks, older homes, yards of reasonable size, and is quiet."

Yet, after seven years, he was still living among strangers. I asked Bill what he might do about it.

"Well, one of my goals," he began, "is to build a network of people—people who you like and who like you, friendly and unpretentious people who can be your surrogate family. I don't have that." If he couldn't find a network like that within the neighborhood—which certainly would be convenient, he acknowledged—then he'd work to build it among a wider circle of colleagues and acquaintances. "I can enjoy most people," he said. "I have the belief that everybody is basically good." Bill paused, adding, "Sometimes, though, people get into a situation or find themselves in circumstances that give them no outlet, like Bob Wills. Clearly he had psychological problems, and probably didn't have the emotional wherewithal to deal with whatever his problem was in a nondestructive way."

Bill pulled onto the expressway. A car cut us off as it swerved to change lanes. "If we were walking on an airport conveyor," mused Bill, "or taking a bus or train, we'd at least see who that person is and maybe he wouldn't act that way. But everyone driving in their separate cars, we move in isolation from each other. It's easy to behave that way to strangers."

THERE was little about the size or signage of Bill's basement office to indicate his authority as the hospital's Associate Director of Pathology and Laboratory Medicine. DR. W. FRICKE, said the sign on the door. KNOCK, THEN ENTER. His office was of modest size, and windowless, similar to those of the ten other staff pathologists. Furnishings included an L-shaped desk and a microscope table. Over the desk hung a framed print of "View of Toledo" by El Greco. "Susan didn't much like the painting at home," he said, "and when I moved in here, there was a hook on the wall, so I brought it in and hung it."

On the back wall, between diplomas, was a framed page from a child's book of *Mad Libs*—those games where kids fill in blanks to make silly sentences. It said, "My dad is as hand-some as blank" and in a child's scrawl was written "movie star." Then "He weighs blank and is blank feet tall," and it said, "50 lbs." and "10 feet." The page was signed "Allison, 6 years old."

Bill looked at a few biopsy slides from a study set—slides from older, interesting cases—and thanks to a two-headed microscope, I had the ability to see what he was seeing: a slice of a lymph node from a seventeen-year-old male, which looked like a circle of purple dots, some overlapping and some larger and darker than others. The dots and the spaces between them formed patterns that reminded me of a kaleidoscope, or a splatter painting. It was a close-up viewing of another world.

Later, I joined Bill at his desk. Another thought had occurred: Was there a connection—perhaps aesthetically—between his interests in pathology and Oriental rugs?

"I'm very much visually oriented," he began, "and ninety percent of pathology is a visual process. With cell and protein patterns, you have to look and interpret them. And with rugs, you look at the curves and geometric figures and you have to ask yourself: Does this design make sense? Do the shades of color have aesthetic appeal?"

He continued, "With the blood patterns, every once in a while you look under the microscope and see something aesthetically appealing. I remember as a resident looking at a pap smear once and thinking it had some of the qualities of Cézanne's painting of Mont Sainte-Victoire, a mountain in southern France. Cézanne was a pre-Cubist. He'd break down landscapes, including mountains, into planes—breaking things up into geometric shapes. The cells on that pap smear had the same quality to me."

I was pretty sure that if Bill Fricke could look at dots on a pap smear and see a Cézanne painting, he must be able to see how the pieces of his own life—wife, children, home, career—fit together to make a beautiful picture, a precious whole. That beautiful picture had captivated me since the evening before when we'd sat together at Sunday dinner. I'd envied it and also felt rebuked by it. Somehow, my wife and I had not seen how precious our own family had been; we'd let the dots of our lives fall off the slide, drop to the ground, and spatter. Yet it was maddening that Bill, with his constant talk about how boring everything was—his home, the routines of family life, work—perhaps was not appreciating all that he had. I hoped, and strongly suspected, that his "boring" talk was just an odd mannerism or a form of self-deprecation born of Midwestern modesty. I wanted to know that in that big Tudor house that anchored my street lived a man who himself was an anchor. It would be a letdown to find that my towering, Lincolnesque neighbor, who could see life and death in a drop of blood, was blind to what was so precious in his own life.

My time in Bill's lab was almost up. On our way in that morning, he'd said I'd have to leave by 8:30 when he had a pathology staff meeting. Just a few minutes remained.

"Bill, you've got this great family and home," I began, "and you seem interested in so many things—pathology, rugs, furniture, music. How can you keep saying your life is boring?"

He looked at me and smiled.

"Well, I say that with a certain amount of dissembling," he began. "Most of us live these mundane lives that we slog through, get to the end of, and then die. But the truth is I'm extraordinarily happy."

"You are? You're happy?" I asked, happy that he was happy.

"Of course, I am," he said. "What does it take, after all, to be happy? Family, career, health, a degree of financial security. I really don't have any complaints—as I said, the only thing I'm looking for is sort of a network of people—that sort of surrogate family you maybe take for granted in a small town. But that's about it. What else could I want?"

"So why do you say everything is so boring?"

He smiled again.

"Well, it's just that on a daily basis, you know, we get up, get the kids up and out, go to work, come home, do homework, fall into bed, and do the same thing all over the next day. I suppose Susan and I could do like some people—many of our neighbors, I'm sure—who go to the lake every weekend, or a weekend of skiing, then to an expensive restaurant for dinner, then to a concert. Or on the weekend they hop a plane to New York to catch a show. Honestly, that would get boring, too, after a while."

And the house on Sandringham, his investments—where did all that fit in?

"The money's just so the kids can grow up and do what they're happy doing. If Allison wants to teach art in college, I'd like her to do that and be able to afford a house and replace her car if it breaks down. But most of what I can give her—an education, a strong sense of family—these don't cost anything."

I'd recently seen Bill give his daughter an extraordinary gift that didn't cost anything. Bill had pledged to Susan's father that he would raise their children Jewish, and he had kept his word. The previous November, Allison Fricke celebrated becoming Bat Mitzvah. I hadn't been invited; at the time the Frickes and I were merely acquaintances. Still, I was curious to see how Bill, who had said of religion that he "didn't believe any of it," would conduct himself at his daughter's Bat Mitzvah service. As a member of the same synagogue, it was entirely appropriate for me to attend.

I arrived at the synagogue a little late and took a seat in the back. Small, slender Allison was already standing in front of the congregation on the raised dais called a *bimah*, ready to read in Biblical Hebrew her assigned portion from the holy scroll—the Torah. She had a quiet little voice, and teenage boys sitting near me were talking and shuffling their feet, so I had to strain to hear.

She started out well enough, but the further Allison went, the more difficult it appeared to be for her. She read more and more slowly, and her voice began to shake. Then she stopped and began softly to weep. I'd been to a lot of Bar and Bat Mitzvah services. Most kids are nervous—I was nervous at my own— but I'd rarely seen someone actually break down and stop. In the synagogue, there was complete silence. All eyes were on the rabbi, seated behind Allison, to see what he would do. But it was Susan, sitting in the front row next to Bill, who made the first move. Up to the *bimah* went Susan to hand her daughter a tissue. In a tiny voice, Allison resumed reading, and managed to make it through that section and the next one, too.

Then it was time for Bill and Susan to stand beside their daughter and make a little speech. Susan spoke first. I strained to hear, but being so far back and with the boys nearby talking and shuffling, I could hardly hear anything she said. Then Bill spoke. His voice was louder and I could make out a few phrases: "a daughter grows up and has a life of her own," and "you grew up too fast."

But then Bill stopped, and began to cry. The congregation again became silent. From a pocket in her dress, Susan retrieved a second tissue and handed it to Bill. He took a deep breath, and continued with his speech. As he did, I could see on Allison the effect of what had happened: her face relaxed and her back straightened. Her father, in breaking down, had made it okay for her to have done the same thing. He may not "believe any of it," but Bill Fricke caught the exact emotion of the moment and, even if inadvertently, had given his daughter the perfect Bat Mitzvah gift. After her parents sat down, she read the rest of the Torah portion in a strong, confident voice. Then she chanted another Bible portion—about Kind David choosing an heir— flawlessly.

BILL had just a moment left before he had to leave for his staff meeting.

He continued, "Really, we don't need any of this stuff we have. A big house is nice. A fancy neighborhood is nice. But I'd be perfectly happy living in just about any area of this general community. We forget the difference between our wants and our needs. When you can't afford to go to Barnes and Noble, well, that's why they have libraries. If you can't afford to downhill ski, there are sledding hills and cross-country skiing. People have fancy houses on the Finger Lakes with powerboats, but there's no way I'd want one of those. You can get in a lake and swim around, and enjoy it without spending a gazillion dollars."

Bill said he and his family planned to spend part of next summer on a small, private lake in Pennsylvania where they were going to build a cabin.

"We looked at log cabins," he said.

Oh, my goodness! My vision of Bill Fricke as Abraham Lincoln might literally come true—he was going to spend the summers in a log cabin.

"They're expensive, though," he said.

Of course, the frugality thing again.

Instead, the Frickes had purchased a 1,100-square-foot modular home.

"Modular houses are great—better than site-built houses," he said. "This one will have false log cabin siding, so it will look like a log cabin."

Bill Fricke in a house that *looks* like a log cabin. That would do.

9

Misdirected Mail

POSTAL carrier Ralph Pascale parked his truck across from the Willses' old house at 52 Sandringham, got out, and walked up the driveway to the front door. As I stood beside the truck watching, I couldn't help thinking that this driveway on which my mailman was so calmly walking was the same one that years earlier the Wills children had run down, screaming into the night.

Earlier, I'd asked Ralph what he remembered of the shootings. "I was watching TV that night," he said, "and, my God, when I saw the interview about the murder-suicide, I couldn't believe it. I knew them casually, like I knew you. I knew she played tennis a lot because when I'd come by in the afternoon, she'd sometimes be doing a little gardening and would still have her tennis outfit on. We'd exchange pleasantries. The husband I didn't see much." A new family lived in the house now. The husband, a building contractor, bought it to fix it up and resell, but ended up liking it enough so that he and his family moved in.

Ralph dropped the mail into a box beside the door, then turned and walked back down the driveway to his truck.

FOR all the years I'd lived on Sandringham as an adult, and for many years before that, Ralph Pascale had delivered the mail. What did he think of the neighborhood? I wondered. What did he know about it that we residents perhaps did not? As I had with Brian Kenyon, the newspaper carrier, I approached Ralph and asked if I could accompany him on his daily rounds. He agreed, but with one limitation that initially disappointed me: I couldn't ride in the truck because it was against Postal Service regulations. As it turned out, though, it was easy enough just to walk alongside the truck because that part of the route I wanted to see—Sandringham Road—Ralph delivered by the method known in postal jargon as "bounding," that is, he parked in the street in front of each house or sometimes pulled up into a driveway, and got out to deliver the mail. Either way, it involved short drives and stops—easy enough to keep up with on foot.

I met Ralph, as we'd planned, on a weekday in mid-October at the far end of Sandringham Road, in front of Bill Fricke's house. The neighborhood was quiet, the street still wet from rain the night before. In the truck, Ralph ran the wipers once against a light mist. He pulled up the Frickes' driveway and stopped in front of the garage. I pictured Bill inside the garage on the next Sunday evening in rubber boots and gloves washing the cars. But now it was Thursday, midafternoon; the Fricke house was quiet and dark. Bill and Susan were at work and the kids were still at school. As Ralph dropped the mail into a box near the side door, I heard from Pumpkin, the Frickes' dog, a weak, obligatory bark.

The 36 houses on Sandringham were just a part of Ralph's daily route, which in total included 211 stops. That sounded like a lot of houses to me, but Ralph said it was less than half the number of stops of a typical postal route in the city. The difference, he explained, is that upscale, suburban neighborhoods get a "ton of mail," often twenty to thirty catalogs plus ten to fifteen letter-size pieces of mail a day. But he wasn't complaining.

Nearly forty years earlier, as a rookie carrier, Ralph's initial postal assignment had been a public housing project. "Back then, you got the worst neighborhoods at first," he explained. Then, during the height of the Vietnam War, at age twenty-two, he was drafted into the Army. When his tour was done, Ralph returned to Rochester and the Postal Service, and was transferred to a blue-collar suburb. Fifteen years later, he was eligible for a new route: Brighton's Houston Barnard Tract.

"I didn't even know where Sandringham Road was," he said. "I took it completely blind. A woman in the office said it was a nice neighborhood with nice people. But when I walked into the station and saw the mail for that route, I was ready to walk out. My other, blue-collar route was working-class people who get the usual type of mail: a bank statement, a catalog or two, maybe a magazine, and one or two letter-size pieces of mail. But yours is a wealthy neighborhood and it's just piles of mail! Tons of financial mail: stock statements, bank statements, circulars, credit card offers, between five and forty catalogs, and on average ten pieces of letter-size mail. It just blew me away."

But he adjusted. "I figured, 'If I'm going to be a mailman, I'm in the right place: gorgeous homes, lovely yards, nice people.' And the first question people ask me when I tell them where my route is, is 'How's Christmas?'"

"So how is Christmas?" I asked Ralph, walking beside the

truck as we approached another house. I tried to recall what I had tipped him last year and hoped it wasn't too far off the average.

"Christmas is very good," he said, "but actually it's good all year-round. For people in your neighborhood, mail is important, and they'll reward for good service."

Over the years, Ralph said, he'd received tickets to the Ryder Cup and PGA golf tournaments "with full hospitality privileges," season tickets to the theater and philharmonic, tickets to Syracuse University basketball games ("a game of my choice—behind the bench"), and an invitation to play golf at the Country Club of Rochester—the club where Deb O'Dell played paddle tennis and a stop on Ralph's route. Customers also sometimes gave Ralph stock tips.

At the home of the stockbroker who had described himself to me as "pathologically private," Ralph pushed an exceptionally large pile of mail through a slot in the back door, along with a treat for the dog. Later, glancing in the back of the truck, I noticed a box of dog treats with a Post-it note stuck to the front that said, "For Ralph, from Tris."

"Who's Tris?" I asked. I couldn't think of anyone in the neighborhood with that name.

Tris was a dog on his route, said Ralph, explaining that dog-owning customers supplied him with nearly all the treats he needed for the neighborhood dogs. He said he hadn't had to buy a box of treats in more than a year. I was embarrassed. Daily, for years, Ralph had slipped my dog a treat but I'd always figured they were supplied by the Postal Service; I'd never given Ralph a box of treats.

Ralph's typical workday began at 7 a.m. with four hours of sorting at the post office followed by four and a half hours of deliveries. I wondered what he thought about while driving the route.

"Much of the time," he said, "I'm thinking about Vietnam vets and ways to recruit more members for our chapter." Ralph chaired the local chapter's membership committee. He also volunteered at the Veteran's Administration hospital, where he ran Bingo games and, as he put it, "brought guys in wheelchairs down for concerts."

An experienced cook, Ralph also liked to think about new recipes. "I look at every cooking magazine that comes through the post office," he said, naming *Cooking Light* and *La Cucina Italiana* as among his favorites. "In the back of magazines, they always have a recipe index. If something catches my eye, I put it aside, make a copy—I still deliver the magazine that day, of course."

A UPS truck passed us coming the other way. "There's the competition," I said. Ralph waved "hello" to the driver.

Over the years, said Ralph, some customers, aware of his interest in cooking, have invited him into their homes to see their kitchens. "I've seen some spectacular houses," he said, eyes wide. He recalled one kitchen with an eight-burner Viking stove. "Right now," he said, "I'd love to be invited into the Gannett house." Once the home of newspaper publisher Frank Gannett, the mansion recently had undergone two years' of remodeling by its new owners, the incoming CEO of Bausch & Lomb Co. and his wife. Ralph said craftsmen working at the house had told him the new kitchen was fabulous.

A few months earlier, I had had the pleasure of enjoying Ralph's cooking. I'd asked him for an interview and he'd invited me to his home—a town house he'd recently rented in another suburb and shared with his twenty-year-old daughter. It was a Sunday afternoon. By the time we were done talking, it was nearly five o'clock and Ralph invited me to stay for dinner.

Ralph's kitchen measured six feet across, leaving just three feet of space to move around between the two counters. It wasn't the kitchen of his dreams, said Ralph, but since he and his wife of thirty-two years recently had separated, it was, at that point, the best he could do. He emptied a box of rigatoni into an eight-quart cooking pot, which he described as a "fifteen-dollar Kmart special that included two chopping boards." In a large pan, he stirred meatballs and sausage.

A sleeveless undershirt showed a fine layer of dark hair on Ralph's powerful arms and shoulders. Years of hauling mail evidently had helped keep him, at age fifty-eight, in good physical shape. A trim mustache and short, graying hair combed straight back added to a neat appearance.

As he chopped celery for a salad, Ralph mentioned he'd spent four hours earlier that day at the VA hospital's new hospice unit with an eighty-two-year-old veteran.

"What do you do with the man for four hours?" I asked.

"Whatever he wants to do, that's what we do," said Ralph. "If he wants to talk, we talk. If he wants to watch TV, we do that."

He said he also visited regularly with a former postal carrier who had retired because of a bad back and then developed diabetes, helping him pay bills and doing light improvements around his house.

We ate in the living room on a card table covered with a green plastic cloth. On a wall nearby hung a poster of Lance Armstrong riding for the U.S. Postal Service in the Tour de France. "He's my hero," said Ralph, who often bicycles for exercise on the weekends.

Throughout the meal, I couldn't shake the irony of dining at my mailman's home even though I'd never been invited into the homes of most of the people who live nearby me. I mentioned this to Ralph.

"I wonder if the people in your neighborhood even know each other," he commented. I said he probably knows the neighbors better than they know each other.

"That's certainly true," he said. "It was made clear to me the first day on the job. My manager said, 'Take a few minutes to talk to the people. You are the only connection for many of them to the neighborhood.' These days, of course, everyone's so concerned about efficiency, they tell us the opposite. 'Hurry up and do the route—don't stop to socialize.' But I still do stop."

He recalled once seeing Grace Field, the woman who walked daily through the neighborhood, drop her purse as she got out of her car. "So I picked up the purse from the street and brought it to her," he said. I asked if he'd talked to her much. "Not really," he said. "I just exchange what I call pleasantries: 'Nice day today,' 'Good day for walking,' that sort of thing."

Ralph, in my opinion, was a top-notch mail carrier, but as on any route, once in a while, I would accidentally receive a neighbor's mail. I was curious about that, and how the other neighbors handled it.

"That's a good question," he said. "More than ninety percent of the time, customers would rather give misdirected mail back to me than walk it over to the person next door."

Anything odd about that? I asked

"Well, growing up, if I got a piece of mail that wasn't mine, I'd just run it over to the right house," he said. Ralph grew up in a blue-collar neighborhood in Rochester. "Thing is," he continued, "the more affluent people are, the more protective they are. They don't want to get involved with their neighbors, and they don't want to take mail over because it's seen as an invasion of privacy both ways: you don't want your mail seen, and you don't want to let your neighbor know you've seen their mail. Also, they just don't want to have to engage in a conversation that maybe they don't want to have."

"Guilty as charged," I thought. Many times when I'd received mail for neighbors, instead of taking it over, I'd given it back to Ralph. It would have felt awkward to show up at the home of someone I barely knew with a bank or stock statement. It'd be socially awkward, too, to meet someone in my neighborhood while, in effect, performing the duties of a mailman.

So why, I asked Ralph, don't neighbors want to know each other?

"Look, at the time of the Depression," he said, "your neighborhood *was* your life because you had no money to do other stuff. Now, there are so many other diversions, especially for the affluent. You got people who belong to two country clubs and are active in the community. There are events they're expected to attend—it's not even an option, it's mandated: 'You will be on the board, et cetera.' Affluent people have so many obligations and so many different avenues for socializing that being part of a neighborhood just doesn't happen."

I was impressed with Ralph's insight; like Brian Kenyon, the newspaper carrier, he had a good read—thanks to years of close contact—on the neighborhood. And I was glad someone in my neighborhood subscribed to *La Cucina Italiana*, because Ralph's rigatoni was delicious.

LATER, it occurred to me that Ralph's knowledge of his customers was, to some extent, a function of the kind of route he had:

by delivering directly to our homes, he often had a chance to meet us at the door, face to face. If he'd had a different kind of route, say, an apartment building where he delivered to a bank of lobby mailboxes, he might see his customers only rarely.

But that's not to say affluent apartment building residents don't have service people who get to know them intimately. They do. They're called doormen.

"[The doorman] has watched [his] tenants for years," writes Peter Bearman, chair of the Department of Sociology at Columbia University, and author of *Doormen*. "He knows their names. If they have kids, he has watched them grow. He knows when they come home, what they do at night, the movies they watch, and what kinds of foods they eat. He knows if they drink. He knows when one of them is having an affair, is in trouble, and when one of their friends is in town. He likely knows their relatives by sight."

This knowledge grows out of the tasks most doormen perform daily. Typically, these include greeting tenants, getting taxis, coordinating workmen and handymen, screening visitors, logging in delivery of newspapers, mail and packages, dry cleaning, video rentals, and food.

As a result, says Bearman, doormen "know a lot about their tenants: what they eat, what movies they watch, whom they spend time with, whether they drink too much, work too much, play with their children, abuse their partner, have kinky sex, are generous or tight, friendly or sour. They infer much of their knowledge from both direct and indirect observation typically extending over many years."

In this sense, the typical doorman is likely to know far more about his tenants than even the most astute mail carrier knows about people on his route. Indeed, notes Bearman, doormen "know things about their tenants' households" that even the tenants themselves don't know. "Does the adolescent daughter have a boyfriend? If so, how often and for how long does he come over for a visit? Does he only arrive when no one is at home? Does the babysitter have visitors after the kids have gone to bed? Does the cleaning lady leave early? Does the husband come home in the middle of the day?"

Some doormen even spend time—typically on the swing or night shifts—helping distraught or lonely tenants in ways that go beyond their job descriptions. Everything from personal problems to a phobic fear of mice can lead to long conversations in the middle of the night with the doorman, who is something of a captive audience, cast in the role of surrogate mate, friend, or therapist.

Despite this level of service, asked whether they would like to live in a doorman building, many doormen say no. "They know just how much they know about their tenants," writes Bearman. "[T]he idea that someone would know that much about them makes them uncomfortable."

AS I continued walking that fall day alongside Ralph's mail truck, we came to the house of a neighbor whose husband recently had passed away. Before he delivered her small bundle of mail, Ralph put it inside a clear plastic bag. "Her mailbox is tiny, and on damp days like this, some of the mail can get wet from the rain," he explained.

As we approached Lou Guzzetta's driveway, Ralph shared a story with me. "So one day I realize I've got in Dr. Guzzetta's mail some pills from the VA," he began, so I say to him, 'Here's your pills from the VA—I didn't know you were a veteran.' And he says, 'I'm a wounded war hero, didn't you know?' I couldn't tell whether he was serious or not. I didn't know how to take it. Then he says, 'Yeah, I got rheumatoid arthritis.'"

I told Ralph what I knew of Lou's experience during the Korean War, and that he did, in fact, have a war-related disability. "But Lou's still in reasonably good health," I added. "What he'd really like is to be more active, to have somebody to take care of."

"I should mention the VA volunteer program to him," said Ralph. "They can always use good people over there."

But I knew Lou would never go for that. I remembered that what he wanted was a person to take care of, one on one, as he had cared for his friend who died of cancer.

Lou wasn't home when Ralph left his mail. It made me wonder if Ralph ever got concerned about some of the older people on his route, especially if he didn't see them for a few days in a row.

"If I have an elderly customer and the mail piles up for more than one day, I want to know why," he said. "I try to find a relative or neighbor and find out what's going on."

"I feel like I'm family to a lot of people," said Ralph. "I'm happy when they get married. I'm sad when they pass on."

At my house, I asked Ralph to deliver the mail as he normally would. I wanted the experience of seeing my mail delivery from his point of view. So Ralph drove up my circular driveway as usual, got out, and pushed a stack of mail—a smaller stack than some of my neighbors received, I now noticed—through a slot in the side door. That turned out to be not so interesting. I'm not sure what insight I had expected.

At Patti DiNitto's house, Ralph left the mail in a box near the side door. He knew Patti had been ill. "I haven't seen her in a while," he told me, "but a couple of months ago she was out in front when I drove up. She was wearing a scarf that covered her hair and part of her face. I hardly recognized her."

Were there times, I wondered, other than checking on elderly residents, when Ralph had helped out some of the neighbors? Hesitantly at first, and then more rapidly as recollections came to mind, Ralph ticked off a list of things he had done over the years for my neighbors. He'd pushed people's cars out of snow—manually pushed because it was against postal regulations to use the truck. He'd helped people carry groceries from their cars. He'd put newspapers and packages in people's houses when they were away—mailed packages as well as those left by others—and in order to do that, several people had given him the secret codes to their alarm systems. He'd found six or seven lost dogs, lured them with treats into his truck, and driven them home. He'd found a woman locked out of her house because the key was stuck in the door so he disassembled the lock, greased it, and replaced it. He once saw a boy fall off his bike and drove to the parents' house to tell them. He found an elderly woman with dementia locked out of her house so he went and got an eight-year-old boy who lived next door, boosted him up through an open window in the back of the house, and lowered him down so the boy could go in and open the front door. He handed the mail once to a woman in her late eighties and, while chatting with her, noticed he couldn't understand a word the woman said. Recognizing the symptoms of a stroke, he called the woman's daughter-in-law to alert her.

Ralph's recitation riveted me, and as he went on, I began to realize that in some ways he was a better neighbor to us than we were to each other.

Unfortunately, my question had distracted Ralph so that

when he finally drove up Deb and Dave O'Dell's driveway and reached in the truck for what should have been their ample stack of mail, there was none. "Oh, my gosh," he said, "I must have misdirected their mail." We doubled back a couple of houses until, from the box near the side door of a house down the street, he recovered the O'Dells' mail, and redelivered it. I wondered, though, had Ralph not caught his error that day, would the people in the other house have given the O'Dells their mail?

10

Connections

ON a lovely day in early spring, as we walked around the block, Patti told me her doctors had found a small tumor in her head. The clinical trials in San Francisco had shown some increase in immune functions, she said, but it wasn't significant. And she wasn't supposed to drive anymore. The tumor, and medication she needed for it, carried a risk of seizures. Clearly, this was a major disappointment. There was no practical way to get around our suburb, or any of the surrounding suburbs, without a car.

Patti seemed tired. Her face and eyelids were puffy. She wore a long brown wig; I hadn't seen her in a wig before. We'd almost made it around the block when we came up to Lou Guzzetta's house. He was in the front yard picking up small sticks and bits of paper. The weather report in that morning's paper said we'd seen the last snows of winter, so I guessed he was doing an early spring cleanup.

I was glad to see Lou outdoors as it gave me the chance I'd

been waiting for to introduce him to Patti. A couple of times over the previous months, I'd mentioned Patti to Lou. I told him she was one of the other neighbors at whose house I'd slept over. I also told him she was divorced with two children, and that she was a radiologist who had diagnosed her own breast cancer. Lou said he had never seen her—despite her having lived five houses down from him on the same side of the street for more than five years. Neither had he heard about her being sick.

I walked with Patti halfway up Lou's driveway. Lou stopped cleaning to come over and meet us. "This is our neighbor, Patti DiNitto," I told him. "I think I mentioned to you Patti's a radiologist."

"Well, I won't tell you what I think of radiologists," Lou said to Patti, "because I don't know you well enough yet!"

Patti seemed to take the cheeky comment good-naturedly.

They chatted a bit—which hospital are you with? What kind of practice? Lou didn't say anything about Patti's health and Patti didn't mention she was no longer working. Yet since they were both physicians, I'm sure Patti understood that Lou could tell by her gait and appearance that she was not well.

That was the first time—the meeting of Patti and Lou on Lou's driveway—that I had introduced two neighbors who previously had been strangers to each other. Clearly, Patti was going to need more help than any one person could offer, and as I thought about this, it occurred to me that the real measure of success of my whole effort would be if someone who previously did not know Patti—and sadly, that included everyone on the street—would join me in helping her out. If that could happen, well, then we would have a real community. And the most obvious pair of neighbors with whom to start, it seemed to me, were the two standing in front of me in Lou's driveway. Lou and Patti didn't know, but I knew—because of the time I'd spent with each of them—that both could find in the other something they needed. Lou needed someone to take care of, as he had cared for his wife and for friends in their last illnesses. And Patti needed taking care of.

At my request, Lou took us through his open garage into the backyard so Patti could see his in-ground pool, which was still covered for the winter. As I expected, he invited Patti's daughters to swim when the weather warmed up. "Come anytime," he said to Patti. "My kids and even my grandchildren are too old and don't use it. Last year I went in, what, three times?"

We said a cordial good-bye and resumed our walk. I wondered about the obstacles in bringing these two neighbors together. Previously, Lou had cared for his wife and for longtime friends. But to him, Patti was a stranger. Until their brief meeting that day, he had never seen her, didn't even know her name. How much might Lou do for someone who was a neighbor, but only a neighbor? And would Patti, who clearly valued her self-reliance, accept help from someone to whom she had no connection other than a street address? And even if each of them was willing, exactly how could I make it happen?

AS I considered these questions, my own connections with neighbors I'd come to know continued to strengthen. In the months following my sleepovers, I had a variety of encounters. Two occurred during the winter months and stand out in my memory. One evening, an hour before guests were due at my house, I called the O'Dells to see if I could borrow salt to melt ice on my front walkway. "Oh, so you're trying out the new system!" Deb exclaimed, referring to our earlier conversation about how unfortunate it was that none of the neighbors borrow things from each other. Deb found a bag of salt in her garage and invited me to take what I needed. Then, a couple of weeks later, I was driving my son, Ben, to school when my car became stuck in deep snow about halfway down the street. While I was trying to shovel it out, many cars pulled out of nearby driveways and passed by as people left for work, but only one person stopped to offer help: Susan Hyman—Bill Fricke's wife. She was unable to push my car out of the snow with hers, but Susan did drive Ben to school for me while I kept shoveling.

MEANWHILE, I was spending more time with Patti, trying to be of what help I could. For a while, we had a standing date on Wednesdays for shopping. I reserved that day to drive her wherever she needed to go, and often we'd have lunch, too. One Wednesday, Patti had a series of errands to do. By midmorning, we were ready for a break. We stopped for a snack at a nearby café. Patti's feet shuffled and her hands shook slightly as she carried her coffee to the table. I also noted her face was puffy and red, and her stomach protruded.

I could see that her energy and stamina were waning.

So, in the mundane setting of a supermarket café, while custodians wiped tables nearby and emptied trash bins, I asked Patti, "Has your attitude toward life changed at all as a result of being ill?"

"It has," she said, putting down her coffee. She seemed to welcome the question. "Just the simple things are so much more important now, like seeing sunlight coming through clouds and I wonder if it is the last time I might see that—not that I think that so much right now, but when I first started chemo. And being with family. Like I say to my mom, 'Let's go out for dinner,' and she says, 'Why?' And I'm like, 'Because it would just be good to all be together around the table.' And I'm so glad I have the girls. What else would there be to live for?"

Being with Patti helped me treasure the time I had with my own children, as well as the new relationship I was enjoying with Marla.

OVER the next few weeks, Patti seemed to grow increasingly weak and confused. She moved slowly, missed appointments, got her dates confused. She was increasingly moody, too. My efforts to help her were sometimes met with an irritation I hadn't seen in her before.

One day, while out walking, I saw her standing on her front lawn.

"I'm locked out of the house," she said.

She said a friend had driven her to a doctor's appointment and then dropped her off at home, but her house key didn't work. Her former husband, with whom she remained on good terms, had a spare key and she'd already left a message at his office for him to bring it over.

She suggested we go to lunch while she waited.

In the car on the way to the restaurant, I had trouble thinking of what to say. Patti was hard to read. I wasn't sure if she was just irritated about being locked out or maybe also dealing with some bad news from the doctor. I asked if she was tired.

"I am," she said.

I took my eyes off the road for a couple of seconds to look at her, trying to gauge her mood. Depressed? Angry? Near tears? Just tired and annoyed?

"Don't stare at me!" she snapped.

I apologized, and said I was only trying to read her mood.

"I'm in a bad mood," she said.

We rode in silence.

THE opportunity to connect two neighbors finally came in the late summer.

"Hey, didn't I tell you to get that mongrel dog out of the neighborhood?! We only allow purebreds here!" Lou Guzzetta was teasing me again as I walked Champ, but where was the shouting coming from? It was a warm Sunday afternoon. I was walking in front of Lou's house, but I couldn't see him.

Then I spotted him. Lou was in his house shouting at me through the open window of the first-floor library, the little corner room on the front of the house where, on the morning after my sleepover, he'd lain on the couch and talked of his childhood, his marriage, and his career as a surgeon.

I approached him across the front lawn and then, when I reached the window, was surprised to see there was no screen; he'd rolled it up to wash the window.

"So how ya been, Lou?" I asked.

He said he felt fine.

Indeed, framed in his first-floor window, he looked well. He wore an old pullover shirt and khaki pants held up with suspenders. The only thing missing from the scene was his miniature schnauzer that always barked at passersby from the corner chair in the library.

"Hey, I'm going food shopping later," I said, trying to be helpful. "Need anything?"

"I shop on Thursdays!" he retorted. "You know that." I asked if he'd be closing his pool soon and if he would need a hand.

"Nah," he said dismissively. "You're an intellectual. I need someone physically strong."

I had to laugh, remembering when at the Y Lou had urged me to do some arm curls so bullies on the beach wouldn't kick sand in my face.

Why that seemed like the right moment, I'm not exactly sure. But there Lou was, standing in front of the open window, and there I was, standing just feet away on his front lawn, and there was nothing between us, no barriers—even the window screen had been rolled up. I took it as a good omen. It had taken some effort over two years to reach this point—connecting two neighbors who previously hadn't known each other—but I decided to pop the question.

"Lou, you know Patti DiNitto can't really drive anymore—" And that's as far as I got because Lou immediately interrupted.

"I'll drive her," he said. "She would be doing me a favor. Understand? My life is zero. I have nothing to do. Tell her I will drive her and she will be doing me the favor. I'll take her food shopping on Thursdays, to stores, whatever. Please tell her it would be a favor to me."

Quickly, I suggested he call Patti—I'd call her first and ask if it'd be okay for me to give him her unlisted home number—but he said no, he didn't want to push himself on her. "Tell her to call me," he said.

THE following Wednesday morning, I left Patti at the entrance to a family restaurant in a nearby suburb and parked the car.

Usually on Wednesdays, Patti and I had lunch and did errands, but that day I had suggested we go out for breakfast. I wanted her to call Lou in my presence and set up a date for them to get together, maybe for him to drive her shopping or to a doctor's appointment.

I had told Patti that Lou would be delighted to help her by driving. She said she appreciated the offer, and was agreeable. But I also knew Patti was unlikely to pick up the phone and call Lou to ask for a ride. She'd only met him that one time on his driveway. Moreover, to Patti, Lou was a senior colleague, a doctor who'd been a successful general surgeon when she was still in medical school. It would have taken a huge leap both of personality and professional protocol for Patti to call Lou and ask him for a ride. Also, given the signs of confusion Patti had shown recently, even if she intended to call Lou, I was concerned she might forget to do so.

The only way to be sure the Lou-Patti connection would be made, I reasoned, was to have Patti call Lou in my presence. Wednesday, however, presented a problem: that was one of Lou's mornings at the Y, and sometimes afterward he went out for lunch or did errands. That's why Patti would need to call Lou early in the morning and why, on that Wednesday, I had asked her for breakfast.

Inside the restaurant, Patti had already been seated at a table near a window. It was a wet day; rain pattered lightly against the glass. She had a good appetite, she said, and ordered eggs, potatoes, and hot turkey sausage. She looked well, too. Her hair had grown in some, her face was less swollen, and her voice was stronger.

When we had finished most of our breakfast, I handed Patti my cell phone.

"I'm pretty sure Lou will be home now," I said. "But later this morning he'll be leaving for his exercise class. This would be a good time to call."

Patti stared blankly at the keypad on the cell phone, and when she moved to push Lou's number, as I recited it, her finger shook slightly—not from nervousness but because, as I'd noticed earlier, she sometimes had a tremor. I took the phone, pushed Lou's number, and handed it back to her.

Lou often would answer his phone in a big voice, as if he were a TV announcer. He'd say something like, "Hello! This is Louis! And how may I help you?" I was only going to hear one side of this conversation, however.

"Hi, Lou!" said Patti. "It's Patti DiNitto."

A pause.

"Okay. Okay. Yeah—works both ways," she said.

"Well, I'm just sitting here at a restaurant with Peter . . ."

"Yeah, well, I don't know yet."

I bet Lou asked her if I was treating.

"Well, look," she said, "I was just wondering if you might be able to do me a favor by helping me out with a ride sometime, 'cause I can't drive right now, I guess Peter mentioned that."

After a short silence, I could see Patti relax, and smile. "Thursday, yeah," she continued. "I have to do a little bit of shopping."

"Yeah, that's good. Yup. What time would you come and get me?"

Here Patti laughed. Whatever he was saying, Lou was charming her.

"Okay, I don't know, like eleven o'clock?"

"Okay, that sounds good."

Patti looked at me. "Do you want to talk to Lou?"

I said I didn't need to.

Here she laughed again. I don't know what Lou said that was so funny, but it was probably at my expense.

"Yeah, I know. He's writing right now."

Patti listened a moment, then laughed again.

"Okay, thanks. See you then. Bye."

Patti handed me back the phone.

"Lou and I have a date for next Thursday," she said, smiling broadly.

LATER, Lou told me it had been a productive day. He and Patti had done a little grocery shopping and then stopped, at Patti's request, at Starbucks. "She knew just what she wanted," said Lou, rolling his eyes—he hadn't grown up with four-dollar coffee: "A mocha ba-boom, ba-bah," he bellowed, and then, imitating Patti's high, soft voice, "but not too much mocha." All in all, he told me, it had been "a wonderful day. What can I say? A very, very wonderful day. It was terrific. I had a great time!"

Lou had been a great help, Patti reported. "It was nice—he even spoke a little Italian with my mother. And I got caught up on all my errands." Then she had a story to tell: She'd asked Lou if he could drive her the next Monday morning to a pedicure appointment, but he said he couldn't because that was one of the mornings he goes to the Y. Patti said, "So Lou says, 'Change the appointment to another day and I'll take you.' But I said, 'It's hard to change these appointments,' and he goes"—and here she dropped her voice to imitate Lou, booming—"'Change the appointment! They'll always give you another one,' and I said, 'How do you know? Have you ever had a pedicure?!'"

Lou helped Patti out on my occasions. He not only drove her wherever she needed to go, he watched out for her safety and became her advocate. Picking her up one day at her house, he spotted something I had missed: over the back stairway that led from the kitchen to the second floor—the one Patti typically used—there was no light. "She comes down those steep stairs and it's dark," he told me. "I told her she needs a light there and it should be on all the time. As it is now, those stairs are just waiting for a fall." Within a week, Patti's brother had installed a light. And later, listening to Patti's accounts of trying to reach her oncologist by phone, Lou realized she sometimes waited up to two days to have a call returned. Intervening with the medical office, he found a direct number for her doctor that Patti could use. Another time, at an appointment with her eye doctor, Lou was annoyed that Patti had to wait forty-five minutes. "I got home," he told me, "and called the ophthalmologist. 'This is Dr. Guzzetta. I was with Patti DiNitto and she's got a lot of problems. It's okay for her to wait fifteen minutes, but not forty-five minutes.' They said, 'Okay, okay, we'll take care of it.' Later," Lou continued, "Patti called to thank me, but I put a stop to that. I said, 'Now, look. Stop thanking me. You are doing me the favor because if I'm not with you, what am I doing? Sitting on my you-know-what in my house, doing nothing. You're making my life for me, don't you understand?'"

Throughout that fall and winter, Lou and I took turns driving Patti to doctors' appointments, shopping, and errands. (In fact, Patti's family and close friends provided most of her rides; Lou and I played a supporting role.)

And once a week or so, Patti would call in midafternoon to say she'd been delayed at an appointment and could I pick up Sarah after school when the bus dropped her off at the house.

One day, when I met her at the bus stop, Sarah wore a pink coat and carried a purple lunch box. She was in first grade.

"Who's your teacher this year?" I asked as I slowly walked

with her the three doors to my house. She had a tiny voice, just like her mother's, and had to say her teacher's name three times before I heard it.

Taking a pen from her coat pocket, Sarah announced she could write her own name. I handed her a sheet of white paper from my notebook. Stopping for a moment to steady the paper on top of her lunch box, she carefully printed in a mix of capital and small letters: "SarAH."

"I can write curvy, too," she said.

I had not realized how much I missed having little girls; mine had somehow grown up.

Often my daughter, Val, was home from high school or my son Ben from middle school, and we would all fix Sarah hot chocolate or sometimes strawberries and whipped cream as an after-school snack. Sometimes, once Patti returned home, Ben would walk little Sarah home—continuing into the next generation the connection that Patti and I had made.

AS Patti's illness progressed, I sometimes thought of her as "Renan Wills in slow motion"—a woman in crisis mostly isolated from her neighbors. It would be redemptive, I felt, if many of the neighbors could come to know Patti and give her and her family support. But I began to fear there might not be enough time for that. I needed to speed things up. If I could just connect Patti with the small group of neighbors to whom I, myself, had recently connected, at least it would be something.

MONTHS earlier, in casual conversation with Deb O'Dell, I'd asked if she knew the woman who lived two doors down from her. "Don't know her name or anything about her," replied Deb. Now, in mid-December, I stopped at Deb's and told her about Patti's situation.

"That must be scary to be there all day by herself," said Deb. She asked if there was any way she could help. Recalling that in high school Deb had been Athlete of the Year and was still active in sports, I mentioned that Patti's thirteen-year-old daughter, Caitlin, was also athletic. "I know she's a skier," I told Deb. "Patti obviously can't take her skiing, though. Would you want to do that sometime?"

Deb said she didn't ski, but said her country club flooded an area around the paddle tennis courts in winter to make a skating rink. "Maybe Patti's daughter would like to go with me," she suggested. "I've got extra skates."

The next time I saw Patti and Caitlin, I mentioned Deb's offer. They both were open to it. It was December and cold, but not freezing cold; it would probably be at least another month before the skating rink opened. At any rate, I'd first need to arrange for Patti and Deb to meet. Patti, however, was going to Florida to spend the Christmas break with her sisters. We agreed that in January, after the holidays, I'd bring Deb over to meet Patti, and then we'd arrange a date for Deb to take Caitlin skating.

As so often is the case, things didn't go quite as planned.

Over New Year's, Patti was hospitalized for nine days. The first time I visited her back home, she had a wheeled walker next to her bed. "I walk like a duck," she said. "They told me to practice with the walker." After that, it was difficult to predict on which days Patti would feel well enough, or be clear-headed enough, for company. There was a Wednesday afternoon in late January when Patti was feeling well and said she'd be glad to have Deb O'Dell come over, but when I called Deb, she was preparing for an out-of-town business meeting the next morning and wouldn't be able to get together until the weekend. On the next Sunday, Deb and I had arranged to visit Patti at 4 p.m., but as I was putting on my coat, Patti called to say she was too tired. I asked if we could try again the next day, and she said maybe. But the next day, when I called to ask if it would be okay to visit with Deb, she said, "I'm just feeling very tired. Maybe in a couple of weeks."

PATTI had never gotten around to furnishing her dining room. Located just off the kitchen on the back of the house, it was empty but for a carpet, which I think was the carpet that had come with the house when she bought it. Once, I asked if she might consider an Oriental rug for that room, and she said that sounded like a good idea, but she didn't know much about Oriental rugs. Neither did I. But I knew someone who did.

On a weekday evening late in January, Bill Fricke rang my doorbell, and as planned, we walked over to Patti's house together. At my suggestion, he had brought two large, illustrated books on Oriental rugs. I had told Bill about Patti's illness and about her interest in possibly buying a rug for her dining room. He said he'd be happy to help out in whatever way he could. Fortunately, Patti had felt well for several days in a row, and readily agreed to have Bill and I come by to talk about rugs.

In Patti's kitchen, Bill, Patti's mother, Elisa, and I stood around the table for a moment waiting for Patti. When she came in, she moved slowly and unsteadily, tightly gripping her walker. She wasn't wearing a wig; her short, brown hair was brushed straight back. Her face was swollen and broad. She wore jeans and a bulky sweater that made her look stocky.

Before we sat down, I suggested Patti show Bill where the rug would go in the dining room. But instead, Patti showed us the living room. There was an old area rug in there, covered, as usual, with play tables, Christmas decorations, and toys. It seemed to me like an odd place for an expensive Oriental rug, but that's where Patti said she wanted it. I guessed she had decided against furnishing the dining room after all.

Bill complimented Patti on the wood paneling and hardwood floors throughout the house.

At the kitchen table, I reminded Patti that Bill was a pathologist. When she was practicing radiology at the breast clinic, she told him, she had sent biopsies to his lab at the hospital.

"We do aspirate and core biopsies since about three years ago," he said.

Later, when I told Bill that Patti had diagnosed her own breast cancer, he said her biopsy would likely have come through his office.

"Actually," Bill told Patti, "your name came up at the lab just yesterday. I got something from the clinic and your name was on it." Probably a patient, they supposed, that Patti had seen some years ago.

"Uh-huh," she said.

Then Bill mentioned the names of three doctors who he knew worked at the breast clinic.

"Sure, uh-huh," Patti said, nodding. The shop talk must have sounded far away to her.

Bill said, "Oh, well, let me tell you about rugs." He wasn't selling anything, he emphasized. He was there just to advise her, and if she got to the point where she wanted to go look at some rugs to buy, he'd be glad to go with her to a local dealer he knew who was honest and had good-quality rugs.

Opening one of the books, Bill said, "I used to buy these just to put on the floor, but now I see them as works of art."

Bill explained the basics of Oriental rugs: different places they are made—Turkey, Azerbaijan, Samarkand; weft and weave; the "quality and aesthetics" of color and style; and how the number of knots per square inch and the tightness of the weave determine thickness, "just like with towels and sheets."

As Bill talked, Patti thumbed—absentmindedly, I thought—through the rug book. Her mother listened silently from a seat nearby.

There was a sense of all of us trying to make this visit work.

When he was done, Bill mentioned again a local dealer he liked.

"Maybe if I found something at that place, you could come over and take a look?" Patti asked.

"I'd be delighted to," said Bill.

We'd only been there maybe twenty-five minutes; it seemed too soon to go. But we didn't want to tire Patti by staying too long, either. Elisa commented on the unusual weather: it was 50 degrees, remarkably mild for January.

"And how about these tragedies, how do you say it—tsunami?" asked Patti.

Weeks before, a tsunami tidal wave had devastated coastal areas of the Indian Ocean with a great loss of life.

"Yeah, and I guess there was an earthquake in California," she added. "Did you see the news reports? There was going to be something on TV about how all these tragedies are linked."

I had planned just to walk with Bill back to his house and then head home, but it was still early in the evening and so mild, and a lovely mist hung over the street which was so pleasant you could feel it on your cheek. Bill and I decided to take a longer walk around the neighborhood.

I asked him, as a doctor, what he made of Patti's condition.

"She's obviously Cushingoid," he said. Cushing's syndrome, he explained, resulted from the heavy use of steroids to keep brain swelling down. It caused "very fine, thin skin" as well as "trunkal obesity." I didn't like hearing Patti spoken of in clinical terms, but at the same time it was interesting to hear that the aspects of her condition I had observed over the past months fit into these neat categories that Bill, as a doctor, easily recognized.

Bill also explained that the tumor in her head was "growing in an enclosed space" and that there was "only so much room for it to expand" before her functioning became impaired. He said it would likely become harder for her to get around. "It will be a gradual debilitation," he said. "She may not be able to walk."

I asked Bill if Patti, as a physician, understood all that.

"Sure," he said, "but people have coping mechanisms. Why redo her house and why the interest in buying rugs? It's part of the way we cope. You can't sit around all day thinking in three months or six months you're going to die. You have to look past that and keep yourself living and interested."

Could Patti recover?

"No," said Bill. "It's a fatal illness. She's going to die."

I had considered the possibility of Patti not recovering, but still, to hear a doctor say it definitively—and I knew Bill was only trying to be honest—stunned me. We walked a few moments in silence.

"As you know," Bill said, "I'm an atheist. I don't believe in a god that has planned this or that, or anybody's illness. It's like the tsunami and the earthquake—it just happened and a hundred and fifty thousand people died. There's no meaning to it; it just happened. All we can do is accept it and support each other."

We had walked a long time together, but finally, back at Bill's house, we said good night. The night was so pleasant, though— and after my conversation with Bill, I had a lot on my mind—so I continued walking. As I passed the other houses on my street, I found I was able to "read" the lights in many of my neighbors' homes; I knew why particular lights were on, and what they meant. At the O'Dells' house, the bright light visible through a basement window meant Deb was probably working out; a light in the second floor study left on past midnight possibly meant she was preparing for a business meeting the next morning. At Patti's, a light at the far end of the house on the second floor usually meant someone—most likely her mother—was staying over to help and sleeping in the guest room. At Bill Fricke's, a light in the corner window of the first floor perhaps meant Bill was reading medical journals; if the kitchen light was on much past 9 p.m., it probably meant Bill or Susan were fixing the kids' lunches, or dinner for the next evening. And at Lou Guzzetta's, I knew the dim light on the second floor was a nightlight and meant Lou was in bed, most likely asleep.

All these lights, and others, taken together formed a sort of constellation for me, a picture of my neighbors inside their homes, living their lives, side by side with mine. Picturing myself as one point of light within that constellation was comforting.

Comforting, too—in what I admit may seem a bizarre way— was the thought, as I walked home, that I was also linked with my neighbors by what went on *under* our street. Some months earlier, I'd learned by chance that engineers for the Town of Brighton used a robotic video camera to inspect the sanitary sewer under the street for cracks. They did this once every ten years, and by the courtesy of our town engineer, I was allowed to view the most recent archived films. On first impression, what I saw on the TV screen at Town Hall looked like a diagnostic video of the human heart. But instead of a cardiac artery, what I saw was the inside of an eight-inch iron pipe into which ran all the wastewater from the homes on Sandringham: water from sinks, dishwashers, toilets, and baths. By gravity, it flowed down the street, joined with the main line to a treatment plant, and then into Lake Ontario, where two miles offshore it was discharged.

On the screen, I saw a churning, reddish-brown liquid; bubbles and bits of paper occasionally floated by. It was a brown soup of shampoo, dish detergent, food scraps, and everything washed off, excreted, and shed by the bodies of my neighbors and me, the ooze of our fleeting existences, the stuff of our middle-of-the-night fears, our own private River Styx. It was what we have most in common: our physical, mortal selves mixed together under the street, flowing by natural force toward the immense, cold lake. This dark mixing of our lives underground was matched, as I thought about it, with the more pleasing, physical world we all shared aboveground. It was something else we all had in common, I thought, this microenvironment of our street. Driving, we passed the same mix of lindens and Douglas firs, the same arrangement of Colonial, Tudor, French Chateau, and contemporary houses, the same harp-shaped streetlamps; walking, we walked on the same sidewalk, avoided the same uneven concrete slabs; in the moment before we turned the corner, our gaze fell on the same houses across the street. On a summer night, if our windows were open, we fell asleep to the same sound of crickets; in the morning, we awoke to the same bird-

neighborhood continually for more than an hour, replaying the relationship in my mind.

I hadn't been out in the neighborhood that early since the morning Brian Kenyon picked me up to ride with him as he delivered newspapers. Brian, I could see, had already made his rounds; at most of the homes I passed, blue plastic newspaper bags rested on the doorsteps. A mist hung over the street. As the sky lightened, birds sang. Their singing was loud, and sustained. Robins and mourning doves I could identify; I didn't know the rest. Then a few joggers appeared. Renan and Bob Wills used to jog together; that's one thing everyone in the neighborhood seemed to remember about them.

I felt more alone than at any time since the days immediately after my wife left. Circling the block in the early morning light, I worked myself into a pretty good panic over the prospect of being alone forever.

At 6:30 a.m., I wondered what I could do to make it to 7:30. Then I saw a light in Lou Guzzetta's kitchen. Maybe he'd come out and walk his dog; I could walk with them—that would oc- cupy twenty minutes or so.

I called Lou on my cell.

"Hi, Lou. It's Peter." I was about to say more, but didn't have to.

"I saw you out walking," said Lou. "You're not usually up this early. What's going on? Do you want to come in?"

I wanted very much to come in.

My face must have revealed fatigue and anxiety because as soon as Lou saw me, he asked what the matter was.

"Woman troubles . . . my friend said good-bye," I mumbled. Previously, I'd told Lou about my relationship with Marla.

"You're a mush-mush!" he scolded. "You let these women

walk all over you. Show some backbone! *Madone!* She was no good. I say, 'Good riddance—you dodged a bullet!'" Then he asked if I'd had anything to eat. I said I wasn't hungry but he told me to have a seat.

I sat at the table in the little alcove in the front of Lou's kitchen. Through the sheer cloth curtain that his wife, Edie, had made, I saw more joggers and a few cars pass. Lou's dog came over and jumped on my leg. It felt good to pet her.

Lou put a plate of toast in front of me, along with jam and butter, and orange juice.

"It's white bread," he said. "I haven't got that whole wheat, nine-grain ba-boom, ba-bah you eat . . ."

As I ate, I told Lou more about what had happened.

He listened, then said, "I'm not a counselor or trained professional. I don't know what to tell you to do." He said this in a tone that was quieter, calmer, and more soothing than any I'd heard him use before.

When I was done, Lou said, "You look like shit—pardon my French. Have you slept at all?" I said I'd slept a few hours.

"You need to rest," he said, and excused himself from the kitchen for a moment. He came back with a bottle of Tylenol PM. "For pain and sleep," he read from the label. "That would seem to cover it." He told me to take two.

"Are you alone in the house?" he asked. I said I was. "That's tough—the being alone."

"Maybe I could lie down?" I asked.

"Of course, anywhere you like," he said. "Living room? Library? Upstairs?"

He said if I wanted, I could stay all day. "I'll be here. I'm not going anywhere. What else have I got to do?"

I thanked him.

"No, don't thank me!" he said. "You'll be doing me a favor. I'm all alone here. Just the dog and the fish."

At the top of the stairs I turned left toward the corner room that had once been shared by two of Lou's daughters. The night I'd slept over, it had been my room.

It looked exactly the same: twin beds, shag carpet, and on matching dressers, model boats and planes that Lou had made.

In that quiet moment I was able to think about what had happened that morning. I'd been bereft, fatigued, and a little panicky, and in that moment of need, I'd seen a light in my neighbor's house. Since that first sleepover, Lou and I had come to know each other well enough for me to call him, and for him to invite me in, and for me to accept the invitation.

I didn't know it that first morning, but for the next week or two—as I absorbed the shock of the breakup—Lou and I would share breakfast at his house almost daily. He was a good listener. He didn't try to tell me what to do, although I got plenty of pep talks. "Be strong. Don't be a mush-mush!" he'd say again and again. In turn, I taught him a few things. One morning, Lou bought—"in my honor," as he said— bagels, lox, and cream cheese, but admitted he didn't know how to serve them. "Do you eat it all together or do you eat the lox separately?" he asked. I showed him how to put a "schmear" of cream cheese on a bagel and top it with lox. Another morning, I brought pancakes, and another day, granola and soymilk—which, to my surprise, he liked. One morning, Lou and I both put on aprons and washed the dog in the kitchen sink. Just knowing every day that when I awoke there'd be someone nearby to have breakfast with was helpful; often, it was enough to get me through the day.

As I lay in that twin bed upstairs at Lou's house, I understood that the community of neighbors I'd set out to find, I had found. There were Lou and Deb and Patti and Bill. There was Jamie, who, with her marriage collapsing, was going through her own troubles. There were Brian and Ralph, bringing us the newspaper in the morning and the mail in the afternoon, and there was Grace, still walking through the neighborhood after all those years.

That it would end up being me who would find shelter at a neighbor's house is something that had never occurred to me when I started my journey, yet there it was. I was grateful to Lou for the breakfast he provided me that morning, for the bed he allowed me to rest in, and—in a larger sense—for the sustenance he provided. That neighborly support, I now understood, is available to all of us.

I was still resting when Lou knocked and came in. His face was soft—even tender—in a way I hadn't seen before. He held a blanket—it was cold in the room; being so early, the house hadn't warmed yet.

"Dad's got an extra blanket for you," he said.

Lou covered me gently, then left the room and closed the door.

Epilogue

FOLLOWING that morning when Lou took me in, we saw each other often—sometimes daily. We would walk our dogs together; sometimes we would just sit and chat. The back pain Lou suffered gradually worsened. At times, he needed to take four or five pain pills just to get through the day. But he still met his buddies at the Y three mornings a week, still went grocery shopping on Thursdays, and still fixed himself a drink every afternoon around three.

Patti DiNitto didn't do so well. As her disease progressed, she never got the chance to furnish her dining room; instead, in a sad irony, she ended up living in it. When Patti's health deteriorated to the point that she could no longer climb stairs, or even walk unaided, her brother, Joe, set up a hospital bed for her in that room.

One day, before the family had arranged for full-time home health aides, Patti's mother called me to ask if I could come over and stay with Patti for an hour or two while she and Joe did errands. When I arrived, Patti was sleeping so I just sat in a rocking chair beside her bed. The house was still. I thought how strange: here I am, the only person watching over a neighbor who only recently I hadn't even known, and likely never would have known but for the deliberate decision to meet her. If I hadn't done that, Patti would still be lying in this hospital bed in her dining room, but I would be three houses away and know nothing of it.

I saw Patti only a couple of times after that. Then on Thanksgiving night in 2005, while driving back to my house, I saw a police car in her driveway. The officer wouldn't say why he was there, so the next morning I called Joe to ask if everything was okay. That's when he told me, "Patti passed away last night."

Immediately, I called Lou.

"It's a blessing," he said. "It had to be."

The next day, Patti's sisters from out of town and other relatives began gathering at her house. Lou and I decided to send some food to them. I was at the supermarket having an Italian Deli Platter made up when Lou called me. "You want to make it a little special?" he asked. "Buy one long-stemmed red rose and have them tape it to the top of the container."

Later, when I called to ask if he was going to the funeral, Lou said no—his back hurt too much and, besides, it would be too sad. But early on Sunday morning, the day of the funeral, Lou called me.

"I'll pick you up at ten thirty," he said. "We'll go together."

The funeral mass was held at a Catholic church in a neighboring suburb. All the family members, including daughters Caitlin and Sarah, wore pink breast cancer ribbons on their blouses and jackets. A family friend spoke of the "courage, dedication, and discipline" it had taken for Patti to become a physician. "There was a steel, a fire in her that we shouldn't forget," he said. He closed with a prayer for Patti's daughters, whom he called her "greatest accomplishment."

"It's a hard day for these two," he said. "They have to let go of their mother."

Patti's white casket was wheeled out of the church toward a waiting white hearse as they played a recording of Sarah McLachlan's "I Will Remember You." After the formal rituals of the funeral mass, this song, sung in the first person as if Patti herself were asking the question, hit me hard. I hadn't cried during the service, but I left the church in tears.

In a steady rain, Lou and I walked across the parking lot to his car.

"I never thought to ask," said Lou. "How did you meet Patti?"

I don't recall exactly what I answered Lou, but the truth is, I met Patti deliberately. I met her because it troubled me to think that one night, my neighbor Renan Wills feared for her safety and the safety of her children, but knew none of her neighbors well enough to seek shelter in our homes. I met Patti because later, I, myself, came to feel isolated among those same neighbors. I met Patti because at some point it seemed both absurd and wasteful to be living unconnected to the people all around me.

"Well, thank you for letting me get to know her, too," Lou said as we got back into his car at the church. "She was a marvelous woman."

FOLLOWING Patti's death, I kept in touch with the various people I'd met from the neighborhood.

One spring day, I walked with Ertem Beckman, Renan Wills's

mother, through Rochester's Highland Park. I wanted to see a tree that had been planted there in Renan's memory. Ertem pointed to a twenty-foot-tall ruby horse chestnut tree. When Renan was little, she explained, a horse chestnut tree grew near Renan's grandparents' home in Point Chautauqua, New York, and it was her favorite. A silver tag around the tree's thin but sturdy trunk read, "In memory of Renan Beckman Wills, MD, beloved daughter, devoted mother, February 26, 1955–February 29, 2000."

The Willses' two children, Emily and Peter, were both attending college and doing well, Ertem told me. And her son, Orhan, the industrial psychologist, recently had moved to Rochester with his family—including his young daughter, Renan—so Ertem and her husband had decided to remain in town.

The last time I saw Grace Field, she was walking, but not in my neighborhood. After another fall, she'd become frail and was using a walker, out for some afternoon exercise in front of her own apartment building, attended by an aide. But Grace still expressed a strong spirit and pleasure in being up and outdoors. In January 2009, Grace died at the age of ninety-four.

Ayesha Mayadas, Renan Wills's best friend, continued her work as a jeweler. However, she and her husband, Bill Kenny, separated, and Ayesha moved near New York City, where she had family and to expand her business. Jean DeHaven and Sandra Arrington, and their husbands—neighbors who had lived on either side of the Willses—both decided at about the same time to downsize. They stayed in the Rochester area but sold their houses on Sandringham and moved to smaller homes.

My next-door neighbor, Deb O'Dell, completed her commitment to the Boston-based consulting company, then left to start her own venture capital firm. Deb and Dave continued their midwinter vacations to the Cayman Islands, and Deb and her sister continued playing, and winning, in the women's paddle tennis league.

Artist and Realtor Jamie Columbus divorced, and moved to another section of Brighton. Her new neighborhood included an example of the kind of public space she advocated: a small, triangular park at the point where three residential streets converge. "The kids ride their bikes there to play baseball, and I can read and watch them play," she told me. The park hosts a Memorial Day parade, Labor Day picnic, and Halloween carnival. "The physical structure of this neighborhood is superior," she said. "As a neighborhood, for me it works well."

Bill Fricke and Susan Hyman invited me to the Bar Mitzvah of their son, Jonathan ("Bubba"). Once again, Bill spoke movingly. "You came with no owner's manual," Bill said publicly to his son. "So I had to learn a lot. I wanted you to grow up to be kind, so I had to learn to be kinder. I wanted you to grow up to be patient, so I had to learn to be more patient." Bill could still hit just the right note.

Newspaper carrier Brian Kenyon gave up his route. A promotion and raise at his day job allowed Brian the luxury of sleeping through the night and enjoying more time with his family. And Ralph Pascale, after delivering the mail on Sandringham for so many years, retired. Ralph continued his volunteer work with Vietnam vets and the local VA hospital.

In April 2008, Lou Guzzetta died in his sleep, at home. He was eighty-six years old. A funeral mass was held at the same church where more than fifty years earlier Lou and Edie had married. I was honored to serve as a pall bearer. The obituary in the local paper said: "Lou served his country as a surgeon with the Marine Corps; his community as a dedicated, skilled physician; his family as a proud and loving husband and father; and all who knew him as a charming, often challenging, always caring, and ever sweet companion, neighbor, and friend."

A week or so later, as they began cleaning out the house in preparation for sale, Lou's children generously invited me to take anything I wanted in remembrance. I walked slowly through the house, revisiting all the rooms where Lou and I had spent so much time. In the end, I accepted just a few personal items: a tie, a pair of slippers, a wristwatch. But really, I didn't need anything; Lou had already given me so much.

THE community of neighbors that I'd set out to find, I had found. Had I not undertaken the deliberate effort to meet them, I would never have known Lou Guzzetta's wisdom, or Deb O'Dell's talent and energy, or Jamie Columbus's artistry, or Bill Fricke's quiet strength of character. And I would have missed the chance, by embracing Patti DiNitto, to try to redeem in a small way our neighborhood's failure to have known Renan Wills.

In all, I had contact in one way or another with nearly half of the thirty-six households on my street. Most neighbors, I'd learned, wanted more or less the same thing: to live among others with a sense of common humanity, expressed through a willingness to know and be known. Even the ones who had declined to cooperate with me had expressed much the same desire. I'd also learned that at times there is just no substitute for a neighbor close at hand. Friends at work or at church or at the tennis club are fine, but a friend even minutes away can be a friend too far. Lou Guzzetta's daughter lived just twenty minutes away. Renan's friend Ayesha lived fifteen minutes away. Fifteen or twenty minutes can be a long time when you're stuck in bed in the middle of the night with a back spasm, as Lou had been, or when your husband is downstairs feeding mortgage papers into the fire.

Did the neighborhood change at all through my efforts? For those I came to know well, and introduced to each other, I think there developed a greater sense of community. How many ripples spread out from that core group? I can't say; perhaps time will tell. I'm not sure if I'll be here, though. My son, Ben, is nearing college age and already this house feels too big; soon it will be time for me to downsize.

But I'll leave with wonderful memories. Coming to know each of these neighbors has enriched my life; it was an experience I've been eager to share.

In June 2008, I wrote an essay about it, which was published as an Op-Ed in the *New York Times* under the title, "Won't You Be My Neighbor?" It seemed to hit a nerve. Readers responded with hundreds of comments and letters to me, and for a time it was among the paper's most frequently e-mailed columns. The comments were overwhelmingly positive. They came from India, Oman, Germany, England, France, Mexico, Canada, and many of the fifty states. Some of those responding lamented the loss of close neighborhood ties; others recounted happy memories of growing up in friendlier neighborhoods than the ones they now live in. And many wanted to share inventive ways they'd found to improve their own neighborhoods:

• In Old Oaks, an area east of downtown Columbus, Ohio, neighbors take turns hosting "Wednesdays on the Porch." These are social hours where neighbors come to chat. As a result, wrote Doug Motz, "my family and friends are consistently amazed that I know my neighbors, they know me and we have an involvement in each others' lives that goes beyond fences."

• In San Rafael, California, after years of "scarcely knowing" their neighbors, Mike Van Horn and his wife began hosting annual parties for their neighbors, a practice other neighbors have taken up. The parties now draw thirty to forty people. "These shindigs have clearly strengthened our local neighborhood," wrote Mike, "and we now live within an expanding circle of friends, not strangers."

• To follow up a block party in his neighborhood close to downtown Portland, Oregon, Dennis Maxwell created a neighborhood map showing locations of the families, names, children, pets, telephone numbers, and work numbers for emergencies. All new residents get a map. "We exchange child care, take care of mail [and] newspapers, and water plants during vacations," reported Maxwell. Neighbors have also exchanged keys to help when people are locked out. "This neighborhood really works for us," he added.

• In ten communities in Oregon, photographer Julie Keefe joined with middle school students to interview and photograph neighbors as part of a statewide arts project called "Hello Neighbor." Then they hung mural-size black-and-white photographs with text throughout the communities to introduce the neighborhood to its children and neighbors to each other. (For more on this project, sponsored by the Caldera arts organization, visit www.helloneighborproject.org.)

• In Marne, France, neighbors hold *fête des voisins* ("neighbors' eve") when, as described by resident Veronique Masson, people gather in front of their houses and share Champagne, pizza, cakes, and quiches. "Knowing your neighbor instead of ignoring them is like being a thread in a tapestry," she wrote. "Alone, this thread seems colourless, but put on the loom with other threads, it can become a thing of beauty."

• In Reno, Nevada, the last week in June is "Get to Know Your Neighbor Week," sponsored by the Conscious Community Network. It's a celebration that has generated more than sixty-five simultaneous pot lucks, barbecues, block parties, and other gatherings, with thousands of participants. "Many folks who organize gatherings continue with what we have called 'caring circles' that go year round to connect neighbors to each other," wrote Richard Flyer.

• In a neighborhood north of Oakland, California, on Thursday evenings residents hold an outdoor film festival, showing films on the side of a bank building. "Last week, I wandered down to find over a hundred neighbors gathered, sitting on lawn chairs right there in the middle of 49th street, watching a series of short films together," wrote a resident named Ian. "What a success!"

• In Pelham, New York, Anne Jacobi hosts "coffees" to introduce neighbors on her block, something she has done for nine years. "I suggest it to anyone, as it is easy to host," she wrote. "You just need a coffeepot, muffins and cookies, and a welcoming mat!"

• From Philadelphia, a woman named Renee wrote, "If you are a bit on the shy side, start a garden in front of your house and plant yourself out there. Neighbors I knew only by sight now see my outside and stop by to chat. Make yourself available and you will be surprised what doors—and hearts—will open."

* * *

RECENT U.S. Census data show that 22 percent of the homes and 38 percent of the apartments in this country are occupied by just one person. That works out to nearly 30 million people living alone, a higher number than ever before recorded. Add to that an economic recession that often puts travel and paid entertainment out of reach. So if there was ever a good time to break down the barriers that separate us from our neighbors and instead take advantage of the potential for companionship close at hand, that time is now.

To do so, we really don't need to sleep over at each other's houses. All we need to do is deliberately set out to know the person next door, or across the street, or down the block; to ring the bell and open the door.

ONE other person wrote me. She identified herself only as Pamela, from Jackson, Mississippi. "Knowing your neighbors," she wrote, "means when a truck backs up to your house, they know you aren't moving and call the police. Knowing your neighbors means when your car doesn't move for a day or two, they get worried and come see if you're okay. Knowing your neighbors means when the ambulance comes to the house down the street, you know you can help without waiting to be asked. Yes, we all have family and friends, but neighbors are special: they are people who look out for you every day because they are there every day; they are people you can look out for every day because you care. If we all cared about our neighbors, we could change the world one street at a time."

Mumford, Lewis. *The City in History* (New York: Harcourt, Brace & World, 1961), p. 512.

Onyx, Jenny, and Paul Bullen. "Measuring Social Capital in Five Communities in NSW," *Journal of Applied Behavioral Science* 36, no. 1 (March 2000): p. 23 and App., Part D.

Putnam, Robert. *Bowling Alone* (New York: Simon & Schuster, 2000), p. 19.

Rose, Reginald. "The Incredible World of Horace Ford," season 4, episode 117, *The Twilight Zone*, directed by Abner Biberman, original air date: April 18, 1963.

Wellman, Barry, and Keith Hampton. "Living Networked in a Wired World," *Contemporary Sociology* 28, no. 6 (November 1999).

SOURCES/RESOURCES

Bearman, Peter. *Doormen* (Chicago: University of Chicago Press, 2005), pp. 6, 66, 95, 121, 124.

Brayer, Betsy. "Who Was Houston Barnard?" *Historic Brighton News* 1, no. 2 (Fall 2000): 7.

Duany, Andres, Elizabeth Plater-Zyberk, and Jeff Speck. *Suburban Nation* (New York: North Point Press, 2000), pp. 40–41.

Earle, Alice Morse. *Home Life in Colonial Days* (New York: The Macmillan Co., 1898), pp. 388, 390.

Finn, Marcia Hibbs, ed. *A History of the Town of Brighton, 1814–1989* (Monroe County, NY: 175th Anniversary Committee, 1989).

Gottlieb, Jane. "Growing Together," *Real Simple*, June 2007.

Hampton, Keith, and Barry Wellman. "Neighboring in Netville: How the Internet Supports Community and Social Capital in a Wired Suburb," *City & Community* 2, no. 4 (December 2003).

Keats, John. *The Crack in the Picture Window* (New York: Houghton Mifflin Co., 1956).

Jackson, Kenneth T. *Crabgrass Frontier: The Suburbanization of the United States* (New York: Oxford University Press, 1985), p. 250.

Latson, Jennifer. "Isle Neighbors Prevail by Banding Together," *The Houston Chronicle*, September 22, 2008.

Liukkonen, Petri. "Biography of Conrad Aiken." Available online at www.americanpoems.com/poets/Conrad-Aiken.